Gun-guwelamagapa

The Land of Our Old People

TOM AUSTEN BROWN STUDIES IN AUSTRALASIAN ARCHAEOLOGY

Dr Tristen Jones, Series Editor

The Tom Austen Brown Studies in Australasian Archaeology series publishes new research on the archaeology of Australia and the adjacent regions. It aims to develop our understanding of Australasia's human past, with particular focus on the archaeology of Aboriginal and Torres Strait Islander peoples during both prehistoric and contact periods.

Animal Bones in Australian Archaeology: A Field Guide to Common Native and Introduced Species
Melanie Fillios and Natalie Blake

Between the Murray and the Sea: Aboriginal Archaeology in Southeastern Australia
David Frankel

Crafting Country: Aboriginal Archaeology in the Eastern Chichester Range, North-West Australia
Caroline Bird and James W. Rhoads

Gun-guwelamagapa: Gun-nerranga gun-nerranga rrawa, An-barra gun-nika
The Land of Our Old People: All the different camps on An-barra *Country*
Betty Meehan, Rhys Jones, Sally Brockwell, Betty Ngurrpangurrpa and the *An-barra* Community

Jakarda Wuka (Too Many Stories): Narratives of Rock Art from Yanyuwa Country in Northern Australia's Gulf of Carpentaria
li-Yanyuwa li-Wirdiwalangu (Yanyuwa Elders), Liam M. Brady, John Bradley and Amanda Kearney

Photogrammetry for Archaeological Objects: A Manual
Madeline G.P. Robinson

Gun-guwelamagapa

Gun-nerranga gun-nerranga rrawa, An-barra gun-nika

The Land of Our Old People

All the different camps on *An-barra* Country

Betty Meehan, Rhys Jones, Sally Brockwell, Betty Ngurrpangurrpa and the *An-barra* Community

SYDNEY UNIVERSITY PRESS

First published by Sydney University Press

Sydney University Press
Fisher Library F03
Gadigal Country
University of Sydney NSW 2006
AUSTRALIA
sup.info@sydney.edu.au
sydneyuniversitypress.com

A catalogue record for this book is available from the National Library of Australia.

ISBN 9781761540202 paperback
ISBN 9781761540394 hardback
ISBN 9781761540219 epub
ISBN 9781761540196 pdf

Cover image: Aerial view of the mouth of *An-gartcha* Wana (Blyth River, NT) 1959 (NT Land Surveys Department).

We acknowledge the traditional owners of the lands on which Sydney University Press is located, the Gadigal people of the Eora Nation, and we pay our respects to the knowledge embedded forever within the Aboriginal Custodianship of Country.

Aboriginal and Torres Strait Islander readers are advised that this publication contains names and images of people who have died.

CONTENTS

List of maps vii

List of figures ix

List of tables xi

Acknowledgements xiii

A note on orthography xv

Background xix

1 Introduction 1

2 Study area and methodology 11

3 Archaeological sites 25

4 Discussion and conclusion 73

5 For the *An-barra:* Text in English (Betty Meehan) 87

For the *An-barra:* Text in Gu-jingarliya 97

References 107

Appendix 1 *An-barra* bibliography 121

Appendix 2 Shellfish resources 127

Index 129

LIST OF MAPS

Map 1.1. Study area location map. 2

Map 2.1. Geomorphological sample sites. 14

Map 2.2. Environmental zones. 19

Map 3.1. Archaeological sites. 26

Map 5.1. Maningrida, NT to Canberra, ACT. 88

LIST OF FIGURES

Figure 2.1. Aerial view of *An-gartcha Wana.* 12
Figure 2.2. Maningrida visit 2015. 22
Figure 3.1. *Aningarra*'s Camp shellfish (MNI/kg deposit). 31
Figure 3.2. *Aningarra*'s Camp shellfish (NISP). 31
Figure 3.3. *Aningarra*'s Camp shellfish weight (g). 31
Figure 3.4. *Gulukula* 2015. 32
Figure 3.5. *Guna-jengga.* 37
Figure 3.6. Rhys Jones in the *Guna-jengga* section. 39
Figure 3.7. *Guna-jengga* Shellfish habitat NISP, MNI & Wt (g). 40
Figure 3.8. Rhys Jones at the location of *Ji-bena.* 42
Figure 3.9. Rhys Jones at *Ji-bena* earth mound. 42
Figure 3.10. *Ji-bena* excavation. 43
Figure 3.11. *Ji-bena* section. 43
Figure 3.12. *Ji-bena* Chronological distribution of shellfish (MNI/m^3). 46
Figure 3.13. *Ji-bena* Chronological distribution of bone (wt g/m^3). 47
Figure 3.14. *Ji-bena* Chronological distribution of fauna by habitat (NISP). 49
Figure 3.15. *Ji-bena* Chronological distribution of stone artefacts (no./m^3). 50
Figure 3.16. Bethune Carmichael at *Jinawunya.* 51
Figure 3.17. *Jurnaka* Distribution of shellfish taxa by habitat (MNI). 53
Figure 3.18. *Lorrkon a-jirrapa* West 1978 Shellfish by habitat (MNI/kg deposit). 58
Figure 3.19. Rhys Jones at the *Muyu a-jirrapa* Coastal Shell Midden. 62
Figure 3.20. *An-barra* children sorting finds at *Muyu a-jirrapa* Shell Mound. 62

Figure 3.21. *Muyu a-jirrapa* Coastal Shell Midden 1978 survey. 63

Figure 3.22. *An-barra* children at *Muyu a-jirrapa* Coastal Shell Midden 1978 excavation. 63

Figure 3.23. *Muyu a-jirrapa* Coastal Shell Midden 1978 Shellfish by habitat (MNI/kg). 65

Figure 3.24. *Muyu a-jirrapa* Shell Mound 1974 sampling. 69

Figure 5.1. Betty collecting shellfish early in the wet season of 1973. 88

Figure 5.2. Students attending Maningrida School 1958. 89

Figure 5.3. Left to right: Three unidentified individuals, art collector Dorothy Bennett, Les Hiatt and Betty Meehan [formerly Hiatt]. 91

Figure 5.4. Nancy Bandieyama with Betty Ngurrpangurrpa as a baby 1960. 91

Figure 5.5. The translation team. Left to right: Shereen Ankin, Ernie Burama, Elva Gindjerakama, Dominic Mason and Betty Ngurrpangurrpa. 98

LIST OF TABLES

Table 2.1. *An-gartcha Wana* geomorphology dates. 15

Table 2.2. *An-gartcha Wana* geomorphology phases. 16

Table 3.1. Dates for *An-gartcha Wana* archaeological sites. 28

Table 3.2. *Aningarra*'s Camp Shellfish taxa (MNI). 30

Table 3.3. *Gulukula* 1974 Bags 1 & 2 Shellfish taxa MNI, NISP & Wt (g). 34

Table 3.4. *Gulukula* 1978 Shellfish taxa NISP, MNI & Wt (g). 35

Table 3.5. *Gulukula* 1974 and 1978 Comparison of shellfish taxa by habitat (MNI). 35

Table 3.6. *Guna-jengga* Shellfish taxa NISP, MNI & Wt (g). 40

Table 3.7. *Ji-bena* Quantitative data. 44

Table 3.8. *Ji-bena* Total shellfish taxa MNI & Wt (g). 45

Table 3.9. *Ji-bena* Chronological distribution of bone (g/m^3 of deposit). 47

Table 3.10. *Ji-bena* Chronological distribution of vertebrate fauna (g/m^3 of deposit). 48

Table 3.11. *Ji-bena* Chronological distribution of stone artefacts (no. & g/m^3 of deposit). 49

Table 3.12. *Ji-bena* Chronological distribution of lithic raw materials (nos). 50

Table 3.13. *Jurnaka* 1978 Bags 1, 2 & 3 Distribution of shellfish taxa NISP, MNI, Wt (g). 54

Table 3.14. *Lorrkon a-jirrapa* East & West 1974 Shellfish taxa NISP, MNI & Wt (g). 55

Table 3.15. *Lorrkon a-jirrapa* West 1978 Distribution of shellfish taxa NISP, MNI & Wt (g). 59

Table 3.16. *Mu-garnbal* Bags 1 & 2 Shellfish taxa NISP, MNI & Wt (g) XU. 60
Table 3.17. *Muyu a-jirrapa* Coastal Shell Midden 1978 Distribution of shellfish taxa (MNI). 66
Table 3.18. *Muyu a-jirrapa* Coastal Shell Midden 1978 Distribution of shellfish taxa Wt (g). 67
Table 3.19. *Ngarli ji-bama* Shellfish taxa NISP, MNI & Wt (g). 71
Table 3.20. *Yuluk a-jirrapa* Shellfish taxa (% MNI). 71

ACKNOWLEDGEMENTS

We would like to thank the *An-barra* community, who own land around the mouth of *An-gartcha Wana* (Blyth River) in central Arnhem Land, for welcoming researchers into their community from 1958 up to the present and especially for participating with enthusiasm in the *An-barra* Archaeological Project described in this publication. Over many years, one *An-barra* family has played a major role in this process: Frank Gurrmanamana (deceased), his wife, Nancy Bandeiyama (deceased), and their five children (two of whom are also deceased). Following the death of her parents, one of their daughters, Betty Ngurrpangurrpa, has enthusiastically embraced involvement in the project. Betty's husband, Dominic Mason, has also been generous with his time and knowledge. Other members of the *An-barra* community (including many children, who were very skilled at sorting shellfish and animal bones into species) observed or participated in the archaeological investigations. Lenna Menzies (deceased) from Tasmania also participated in the excavations at *Ji-bena*. Shireen Ankin, Ernie Burama, Elva Gindjerakama, Doreen Jinggarrbarra, Dominic Mason, Betty Ngurrpangurrpa and Freda Wyartja, with consultant linguist Margaret Carew, translated the community report included in this publication.

In addition, we have benefited by having access to excellent research carried out by other scholars with the *An-barra* community over decades – Les Hiatt, Rhys Jones and John Chappell in particular (some of their publications are listed in the References).

We would like to thank the Australian Institute of Aboriginal and Torres Strait Islander Studies (AIATSIS) for funding the analysis of the *An-barra* archaeological assemblages and our travel to Maningrida in 2003, and the Australian National University (ANU) for providing office and laboratory space. An Australian Research Council (ARC) Discovery Project (DP120100512) funded a second trip to Maningrida in 2015.

Dr Ella Ussher assisted with the shell analysis. Dr Richard Willan (Curator Emeritus of Molluscs) of the Museum and Art Gallery of the Northern Territory (MAGNT) identified shellfish specimens, checked Appendix 2 and assisted with the repatriation of the *An-barra* archaeological collection. The archaeological material from the *An-gartcha Wana* sites is now stored at MAGNT in Darwin. Carto-GIS and Adam Black drew the maps and formatted the tables and figures. Dr Billy Ó Foghlú calibrated the dates, adapted Betty and Rhys' section drawings from the excavation at *Ji-bena* and created the geomorphology map from John Chappell's "mud map". Thanks also to two anonymous reviewers who made helpful suggestions.

We have sought permission from *An-barra* people to use their photographs in this publication. In some cases, they were unable to remember the names of some of the children because these were taken so long ago (and I had not fully documented them in my field notes), sometimes before some of the people I consulted were born! All the people I consulted were pleased to see the images and delighted that they would appear in the publication. Owners of the photographs are acknowledged in the captions. Please be aware that this publication contains images of people who have passed away.

A NOTE ON ORTHOGRAPHY

Throughout this publication, we use words from the language spoken by the *An-barra* community. Where possible, we have used the dictionary compiled by Kathleen Glasgow (1994) and advice from Margaret Carew (consultant linguist) to update some of the spellings of *An-barra* words.

However, where we have quoted from field notes or publications, we have maintained the spellings recorded by scholars who have worked with the *An-barra* community in the past, including Les Hiatt, Rhys Jones and Betty Meehan. None of these people were trained linguists but did their best to record words as close to the *An-barra* pronunciation as possible.

The people and their language

The *An-barra* are "a regional tribe at the mouth of the Blyth River, which speaks the *Gun-nartpa* dialect" (Glasgow 1994, 38).

An-barra is derived from the term for "mouth of the river" (lit., "base, rear end") and, most interestingly, "*ana-burra aburr-nirra* – the people that live at the base of the river" (Glasgow 1994, 38). *Gu-jingarliya* is the "language name for the *An-barra* and *Martay* dialects". See "*Gidjingali*" below (Glasgow 1994, 290).

It is interesting to note what Les Hiatt said about the same people in 1965: "*Gidjingali* is the term for the language spoken by people who, before the time of my fieldwork, lived south of Cape Stewart and around the mouth of the Blyth River [Map 1.1]. They referred to themselves collectively as 'we' and never by any name. I shall call them the *Gidjingali* for the sake of convenience." (Hiatt 1965, 1, Map 1).

The Glasgow dictionary contains a long entry about "we" (1994, 877–88) and an equally long entry about "us" (1994, 874).

Site names

In this list of site names, the Glasgow and corrected spellings appear first. Other spellings used in field notes and publications are in brackets.

Agajang-guwa (Agadjang-guwa)

Anajerramiwa (Anadjerramiwa)

Anamanba (Anandamamba)

Ana-nganandak (Ananganandark)

An-gartcha Wana (Angatja Wana)

Aningarra

Bolgunirra-gaboiya

Gulukula (Kula Kula)

Guna-jengga (Gunedjanga)

Gupanga (Kopanga)

Guyoyo

Ji-bena (Djibena)

Jilangga a-jirra (Djilangadjerra)

Jinawunya (Djunawunya, Djunawinia)

Jurnaka (Djunaka, Djinaka)

Lalarr gu-jirrapa (Lalar-gadjirrapa, Lalagidjiripa, Lalargedjiripa)

Lorrkon a-jirrapa (Larrakun-adjirrapa)

Madayjapa (Madaidjapa)

Malmilajerra (Malmiladjerra)

Minjambilamirra (Mindjambilamirra)

Mugamandija (Mugamandidja)

Mu-ganarra (Moganarra, Moganara)

Mu-garnbal (Maganbal)

Mu-lela (Milela)

Muyu a-jirrapa (Moiya-adjirripa)

Ngakunal-yorda

Nganyjuwa (Ngandjuwa)

Ngarli ji-bama (Ngalidjibama)

Yuluk a-jirrapa (Yuluk-adjirrapa)

Reference

Glasgow, K. (compiler) (1994). *Burarra – Gun-nartpa Dictionary with English Finder List. Based on the Language Shared by Speakers of the An-barra, Martay and Gun-nartpa Dialects*. Produced with the assistance of the Australian Institute of Aboriginal and Torres Strait Islander Studies and the Maningrida Community Education Centre. Darwin: Summer Institute of Linguistics, Australian Aborigines and Islander Branch.

BACKGROUND

Here, Betty Meehan reflects on her long involvement with the *An-barra* community.

While being aware of the complexity of the names of the Aboriginal groups I have known since 1958, I have usually referred to the Aboriginal community that I have known for many decades as the *An-barra* people or *An-barra* community. They seem to be happy with this. They own land located around the mouth of *An-gartcha Wana* (Blyth River) in central Arnhem Land, Northern Territory (NT).

I first met the *An-barra* people in 1958. After several months stranded in Darwin, Les Hiatt and I boarded Curly Bell's boat, *The Kaprys*, a converted pearling lugger, and set sail for Maningrida. This journey took about four days, the sea was turbulent, and I was seasick for most of the way. However, we arrived safely at Maningrida on a fine, sunny afternoon by which time the sea was calm. A large crowd of people had gathered on the beach to welcome the boat.

Maningrida, which lies some 500 km east of Darwin, is located at the mouth of the Liverpool River in picturesque Boucaut Bay (Map 1.1). The settlement was established by the federal government in 1957 to provide trading and medical services for the Aboriginal people who lived in the area. The Traditional Owners of the country on which Maningrida is located are the *Ndjebbana* but very soon people from other communities, speaking many different languages, including the one spoken by the *An-barra* (*Burarra, Gu-jingarliya*), moved into the settlement – for at least part of each year, usually during the wet season. Today, the town supports well over 2,000 people, including those who live on some 30 homeland centres or outstations located in the Maningrida area.

Les, then an anthropology PhD student at ANU, had come to Maningrida hoping to learn about Aboriginal social life. After a series of negotiations, the

An-barra community decided to welcome us both. A senior *An-barra* man, Frank Gurrmanamana (deceased), his wife, Nancy Bandeiyama (deceased), and their children (two of whom are also deceased) agreed to educate us in *An-barra* ways and, as well, protect us from the dangers of the tropical bush.

While living in Maningrida, apart from being a "tent keeper", I participated as much as I could in the daily life of the *An-barra* community. I had previously worked as a primary school teacher and, in 1958, I also established the first school in Maningrida. From a humble beginning, that school has developed into a flourishing establishment which celebrated its 60th anniversary in 2018.

While Les pursued his research, I spent as much time as I could in the company of *An-barra* women and children – harvesting food from the country surrounding Maningrida and occasionally from traditional *An-barra* land, which lay around the mouth of *An-gartcha Wana* some 40 km to the east. I also attended secular parts of ceremonies and enjoyed the performances of song series, associated dances and the production of beautiful objects manufactured by *An-barra* people for these events and for use in their daily life.

It is hardly surprising that, eventually, after spending two enjoyable years in this unique and stimulating environment, I enrolled as a mature-age student at the University of Sydney, specifically to study anthropology. Fortunately for me, this was the first year that prehistory (now called archaeology) was included in the anthropology curriculum. Studying archaeology and anthropology had a major impact on the future direction of my life and the nature of the research that I would eventually undertake – a focus on the lives of Aboriginal women and children, especially the production of food and the material culture associated with these activities.

I returned to Maningrida during the dry season in 1972 – by then an ANU PhD student – with the archaeologist Rhys Jones, to find that many *An-barra* people had returned to their own estate and were living at *Gupanga* – a significant home base located on the western side of *An-gartcha Wana*, a short distance from its mouth (see Figure 2.1). The *An-barra* were there because they were participating in a ceremony being staged across the river. Rhys and I established a base camp at *Gupanga* but spent most of our time, while the ceremony was in progress, living at *Ngarli ji-bama*. After several months, when the ceremony had finished and visitors from other communities had returned to their own estates, many *An-barra* people decided they would stay on their own land throughout the wet season and agreed that Rhys and I could stay with them. This was a wonderful opportunity for us to be with a group of Aboriginal people living on their own land and harvesting much of their food from that area. The *An-barra* estate is rich in food resources – it contains a large river, much coastline, big areas of mangroves and very productive freshwater floodplains. The downside of living in this rich tropical environment is that, during the wet season, mosquitoes and sand flies make life hell for people not accustomed to such challenging conditions. I am pleased to say that before the 1972–73 wet season began in earnest, the *An-barra* moved from *Gupanga* to an exposed coastal site called *Lalarr gu-jirrapa*. At this significant location, it was wild, wet and windy, but, unless you were foolish enough to enter the surrounding mangroves, the mosquitoes and sand flies were manageable.

While in the field, I was always aware of the archaeological manifestation of my research interests. However, at this time I was focusing on the complex life that the *An-barra* were living on top of their land, rather than what their ancestors had left behind in the archaeological record – usually some shellfish remains, animal bones and a few stone tools. However, during 1972–73, in addition to the work I was documenting on *An-barra* subsistence, Rhys and I were able to carry out several small archaeological investigations, which are described in this monograph.

I also felt, very strongly, that it was such a privilege to be able to carry out archaeology on land where many of the descendants of the people who laid down these archaeological deposits were still living. Of course, I understand that one cannot assume that what can be observed of Aboriginal contemporary life is the same as that represented in the archaeological record – but it can indicate what life might have been like. There are no rock shelters or caves located on *An-barra* territory, as there are in other areas of Australia, where rock art images may enhance the interpretation of what is found in the archaeology. *An-barra* "art" appears on the walls of temporary bark shelters, on human bodies for ceremonies, and on some items of material culture. More recently, of course, bark paintings are produced by some *An-barra*, and these often depict significant information about *An-barra* culture, including religion.

I wrote about my life in the *An-barra* community during 1972–73 in *Shell Bed to Shell Midden* (1982a), based on my PhD research (1975). I then had to find employment. I was lucky enough to find positions that allowed me to maintain my friendship with the *An-barra* community and carry out further archaeological exploration with them on their estate. Rhys and I were able to excavate the large mound at *Ji-bena* and several smaller sites in 1978, also described in this monograph. Unfortunately, Rhys died in 2001 before we had a chance to publish the results of these investigations.

Since 1958, some *An-barra* people have been able to travel south to Sydney or Canberra for special events that involved them personally or for holidays. These days, I maintain regular contact with Betty Ngurrpangurrpa (Frank Gurrmanamana's daughter), now 60 years old, mainly by mobile phone. She, like her mother and father, is a highly intelligent, knowledgeable person, keen to describe and explain aspects of her culture to people (including Europeans or "*balandas*") who are keen to learn.

Sally Brockwell agreed to co-operate with me to process and publish results of the archaeological investigations that Rhys and I had carried out on *An-barra* land over time. We made two trips together to Maningrida and *An-barra* land to the east (4–7 August 2003 and 10–14 August 2015) with Traditional Owner Betty Ngurrpangurrpa, her husband, Dominic Mason, and various other *An-barra* people. These trips were designed to introduce Sally to the *An-barra* people and to enable her to see the sites where the archaeological material came from, collect shells for dating and isotope analysis, and keep the community informed about the archaeological project and the monograph we were hoping to publish.

We are keen to publish these results as they give some idea of when the current *An-barra* estate was first occupied by Aboriginal people. After all, if Aboriginal people have been in Australia for as long as the latest dates indicate, perhaps 65,000 years (Clarkson et. al. 2017), then ancestors of the *An-barra* probably have been too. However, because of the time span and the intricacies of the sea-level changes in northern Australia in particular, it is difficult to describe this process precisely. The archaeological story that Sally and I wish to tell is based on the information we have been able to accumulate. It is certainly not the full story and may not, in some details, even be correct. However, hopefully, it will reveal some exciting clues about when the *An-barra* and their ancestors began to occupy their current estates around the mouth of *An-gartcha Wana*, how they lived in the past, and in what way this story compares with how they live today.

Summary of Betty Meehan's contact with the *An-barra* community: 1958 to the present (August 2025)

1958 and 1960: 20 months at Maningrida in Arnhem Land, NT, with Les Hiatt, where he was carrying out research for his ANU PhD (Hiatt 1965). During 1958, I established the first school at Maningrida.

1970: Carried out a reconnaissance at the mouth of *An-gartcha Wana* in Arnhem Land seeking permission to do some ethnoarchaeological research with the *An-barra* community.

1972–75: Fieldwork with the *An-barra* community carrying out ethnoarchaeological research. Rhys Jones was with me for some of this time.

1978: Five months spent at *An-gartcha Wana* carrying out archaeological research. During this visit, I also provided logistical and technical support for Kim McKenzie of the Australian Institute of Aboriginal Studies (AIAS) who was making the film *Waiting for Harry* (McKenzie 1980) with the *An-barra* community at *Jinawunya*.

1978: Assisted Dr Bryan Keon-Cohen to elicit *An-barra* views about proposed law reform relevant to Aboriginal people (Hanks & Keon-Cohen 1984).

1979: One month of fieldwork with Rhys Jones carrying out archaeological research with the *An-barra* community.

1979: Proposed and assisted with the organisation of the performance of the *An-barra* song series, *Djambidj*, by *An-barra* men Frank Gurrmanamana, Frank Malkorda and Sam Gumugun, which took place at the Goethe Institute in Canberra. A record and booklet commemorating this performance was published by AIAS (Clunies Ross & Wild 1982).

1980: Short trip to *An-barra* community to check on and augment information about plants, especially *Pandanus spiralis* [Screw palm]. The kernels of the woody fruit are eaten and the fronds used to manufacture material culture items, like baskets] (Meehan et al. 1979).

1981–83: With Rhys Jones, assisted Dr Ronald Lampert with preparation of an *An-barra* section that was to be part of the Aboriginal Gallery in the Australian Museum, Sydney. Frank Gurrmanamana and Nancy Bandeiyama came to Sydney to oversee the *An-barra* part of the project.

1982: Facilitated the visit of George Garawun, an Aboriginal artist from Maningrida, when he came to visit Canberra for the opening of the National Gallery of Australia, in which several of his bark paintings were exhibited, and where he was introduced to Her Majesty Queen Elizabeth II.

1982: Assisted with organisation of the performance of the *Rom* ceremony at the AIAS by the *An-barra* community. A film was made, and a book published about this event by the AIAS (Wild 1983, 1986).

1982: Short trip to the *An-barra* community to investigate the processing of toxic plants with Associate Professor Wendy Beck (University of New England).

1983: Short trip to *An-barra* community to collect data about sites situated around the mouth of the *An-gartcha Wana* so they could be listed with the NT Sacred Sites Authority (later the Aboriginal Areas Protection Authority) in Darwin.

1986: Short-term fieldwork for the Northern Land Council with the *An-barra* people concerning the ownership of sites around the mouth of *An-gartcha Wana*.

1986: Several months on an Australian Research Grants Scheme for the "Technology of Subsistence Project" with Dr Neville White (La Trobe University) and Professor Rhys Jones (ANU). Time was spent at several Aboriginal communities in the NT, including with the *An-barra* at *An-gartcha Wana*.

1987: Same as above.

1988: One month spent at Maningrida working in the *Djomi* Museum with *An-barra* and other Aboriginal people.

1988: Organised visit of Betty Ngurrpangurrpa and her son Johnson from Maningrida to the Australian Museum and the ANU to work on artefacts from the *An-barra* culture.

1996: With Dr L.R. Hiatt, prepared an exhibition of black-and-white photographs, taken by both of us of *An-barra* and other people living in the Maningrida area of Arnhem Land in 1958 and 1960, in association with the launching of a volume in honour of Dr Hiatt (Merlan et al. 1997).

1997: Prepared *An-barra* genealogies for proposed Native Title Claim for area of sea adjoining *An-barra* land for the Northern Land Council, Darwin.

2001: Assisted the *An-barra* community to bring their *Rom* ceremony to Canberra at the invitation of AIATSIS. During this time, Betty Ngurrpangurrpa visited Rhys Jones in Canberra Hospital where he was being treated for chronic myeloid leukaemia. He died in September 2001.

2002: Betty Ngurrpangurrpa came to Canberra to attend the launch of the book *People of the Rivermouth* (Gurrmanamana et al. 2002) at the National Museum of Australia (NMA). She spoke on behalf of her father, who was too frail to attend. This volume was a joint venture of NMA and AIATSIS.

2003: Trip to Maningrida to introduce Dr Sally Brockwell to the *An-barra* community and to their land around the mouth of *An-gartcha Wana* with a view to the production of a monograph about the archaeology of that area.

2015: Short trip to consult *An-barra* community about the archaeological research I had carried out there and was now preparing for publication. I was also able to introduce Dr Sally Brockwell to more members of the community as she was to be a major contributor to the monograph. We also collected shells for radiocarbon dating and isotope analysis.

2016: Two *An-barra* people, Betty Ngurrpangurrpa and a young relative, Leah, came to holiday with me for three weeks over the Christmas period.

Note: My husband, Rhys Jones, was diagnosed with leukaemia in the late 1990s, and for much of the time he was very ill and required special care. It was difficult for me during this time to maintain regular physical contact with the *An-barra* community, though by then, many of them had acquired mobile phones, so I could keep them informed about Rhys' health and other matters.

1

INTRODUCTION

The information presented in this volume tells us something about how long and in what way the *An-barra* have occupied their current estate – rich and productive land draped around the mouth of *An-gartcha Wana* (Blyth River – literally Big River) in central Arnhem Land, Australia (Map 1.1).

Limitations

Before we begin the *An-barra* story, it is important to note some shortcomings or gaps in our data. For example, the archaeological surveys have not recorded all the sites on the *An-barra* estate, and we certainly did not obtain radiocarbon dates for all the sites located. Also, some sites belonging to the *An-barra*, their ancestors or other unknown people may have been destroyed or covered by the rising and falling sea levels well-documented for this dynamic coastline. Furthermore, we do not even know for certain that *An-barra* ancestors occupied the sites from which our oldest dates have been obtained. However, given the vast antiquity now recorded for Aboriginal occupation of this continent (see Clarkson et al. 2017), the occupants of current *An-barra* land in the past may well have been *An-barra* ancestors or Aboriginal people of different ancestry.

An-barra occupation

How long have the *An-barra* occupied their current estate? No matter what the definitive answer is to this and other related questions, it is clear from the radiocarbon dates and the nature of current *An-barra* culture that they and possibly their ancestors have lived on their current estate for a very long time. The oldest date we have documented so far from any archaeological site is c. 3,500 years. As already stated, there is no way of knowing for certain just how long the *An-barra* themselves

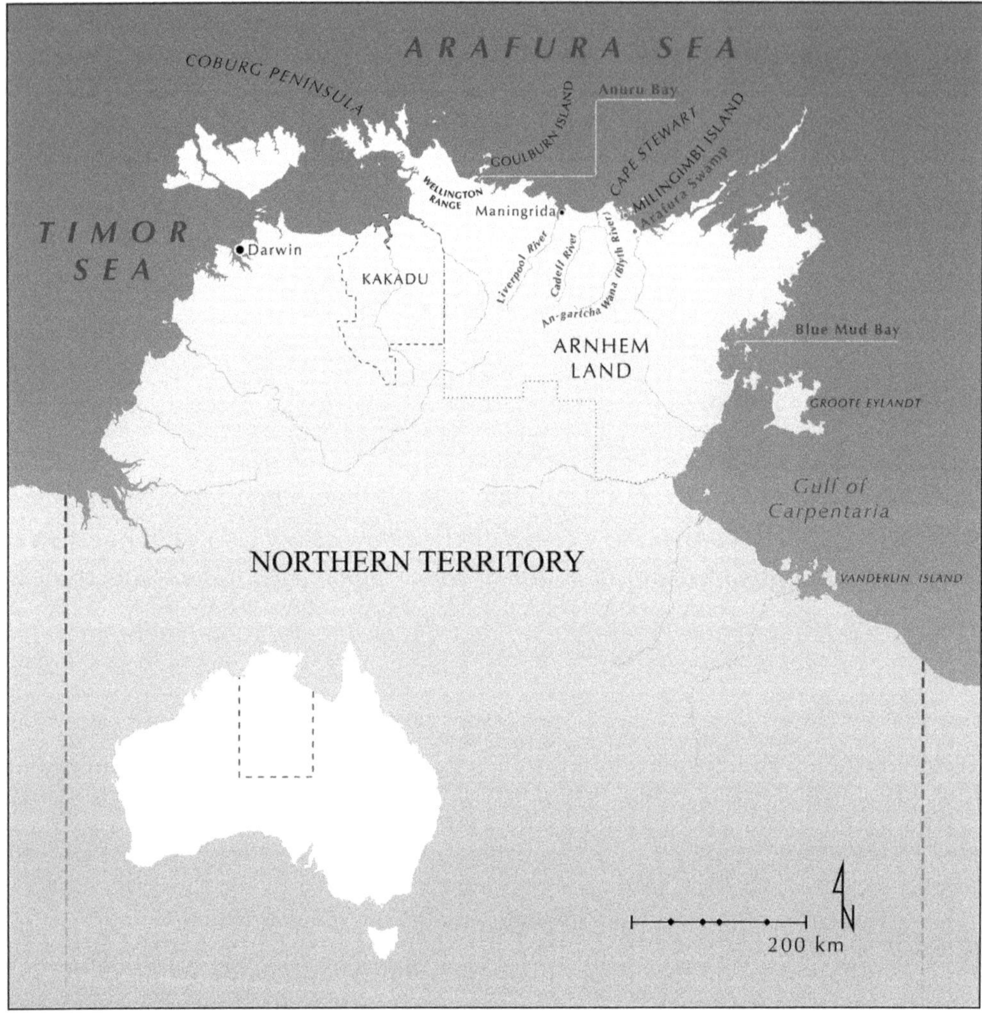

Map 1.1. Study area location map (Adam Black).

have lived on the land at the mouth of *An-gartcha Wana*. No human remains were found (or sought) during fieldwork. In any case, past *An-barra* funerary practices of secondary burial would mean that it is unlikely that human remains would be found in the archaeological record (McKenzie 1980). Nowadays, people are buried in graves at Maningrida or at various places on *An-barra* land – for example, *Ji-bena*.

The complexity of contemporary *An-barra* culture has been recorded by many scholars over past decades – for example, see Glasgow (1994), Hamilton (1981), Hiatt (1965), Jones (1980), McKenzie (1980) and Meehan (1982a) (for a complete bibliography, see Appendix 1). Hiatt (1965) described *An-barra* social life in great detail. This body of research indicates a well-developed and complex culture deeply embedded in the land on which it thrived. Meehan and Jones provide insight into the way the *An-barra* exploit their resource-rich environment to eat well and live healthy lives. *An-barra* people possess detailed knowledge and understanding of the environment in which they live – the coming and going of the seasons including the danger that some seasons (for example, the wet season) may jeopardise their lives – and, of course, the availability of the animals and plants that contribute to their rich and varied diet, and the items of material culture they need to survive (Meehan 1982a).

Their territory is peppered with a great number of named places, many of which also have religious significance attached to them. Religious beliefs and practices are deeply embedded in the land on which the *An-barra* live and suggests that this has been the case for a very long time. The complex art associated with their religious life (both public and secret) is, unfortunately, mostly ephemeral, so leaves little evidence, if any, in the archaeological record – for example, several great song series, such as *Djambitj* and *Goyulan* (Gurrmanamana et al. 2002).

The detailed elements of contemporary *An-barra* life suggest that it is unlikely they are newcomers to the particular piece of land they currently own, occupy, harvest and pay religious reverence to. The complexity of their lives observed by various scholars who have lived with them over decades indicates they and probably their ancestors have been living here for a very long time – possibly far longer than the dates obtained from occupation sites so far indicate.

Historic contacts

It is known that the *An-barra* (or other people who may have occupied their current estate) have probably had contact with various non-Aboriginal people since the seventeenth to eighteenth centuries – Macassans from what is now the Indonesian archipelago; Europeans before 1940; and, finally, more Europeans after the establishment of Maningrida Government Settlement in 1957. Discussion, including references, concerning these contacts can be found in publications by both Hiatt (1965, 5–13) and Meehan (1982a, 16–21). For recent studies on Macassan contact in Arnhem Land, see Clark and May (2013), Wesley et al. (2016) and Xu (2021).

Macassans

It is estimated that Macassans began visiting the Arnhem Land coast from the seventeenth to eighteenth centuries (MacKnight 1976; Urwin et al. 2023; Wesley et al. 2016). They came to collect trepang (*burnapi* in *Gu-jingarliya*) for Chinese merchants in Makassar (provincial capital of present-day South Sulawesi). The Macassans worked mainly in northeast Arnhem Land where rich beds of trepang existed. However, there is some evidence to indicate that the *An-barra* probably had some contact with them during that time.

Hiatt has this to say:

> Old Gidjingali men remember them, but I gather from their accounts that the fishermen did not come regularly to the Blyth River. There is no evidence of Indonesian ancestry among present-day Gidjingali or of changes in social life attributed to Indonesian influences. Yet at some stage several cultural changes occurred. Gidjingali now make canoes from tree trunks instead of bark and smoke long Indonesian-style pipes; they use a representation of an Indonesian mast in one of their ceremonies and refer to the visitors in songs; and the vocabulary includes perhaps a dozen words of Indonesian origin. As these innovations are widespread in Arnhem Land, it is possible that the Gidjingali adopted them from neighbours who had closer contact with the voyagers (1965, 6).

Brady (2013) discusses the introduction of arrack and tobacco to Aboriginal people in Arnhem Land by Macassans well before the First Fleet arrived in Sydney. Mitchell (1996) argues that Macassan introduction of iron and dugout canoes on the Coburg Peninsula in western Arnhem Land enabled the hunting of large marine animals, such as sea turtle and dugong.

The *An-barra* home base called *Gupanga* may well be named after Kupang (formerly Koepang), the provincial capital of the present-day eastern Indonesian province of Nusa Tenggara Timor. Frank Gurrmanamana, always anxious to educate Betty Meehan, drew her attention to a fruit tree, *Tamarindus indica* (called *jambang* by the *An-barra*), which he said had been brought by Macassar visitors, and a waterhole at *Jinawunya*, which he described as "from that *Man-gajerra*" (Meehan 1982a, 16–17).

Australian trepang fishers

In the second half of the nineteenth century, Australian trepang fishers entered the Arnhem Land coast but had difficulty obtaining cheap labour. Apparently, the local people preferred to work for the Indonesians (Hiatt 1965, 5–13; Meehan 1982a, 16–21).

Japanese pearl fishers

Japanese pearl fishing in the Arafura Sea began not long after the Indonesian trepang fishing ceased after 1906 due to an Australian government ban. The Japanese, in general, were not welcomed by the *An-barra*, though several *Gunavidji* (also referred to as *Ndjebbana*) people worked on luggers, and two *Gu-jingarliya* people have Japanese ancestry. Japanese pearl fishing ceased during World War II but began again in 1953 (Gillett 1981; Meehan 1982a, 17–18; Oliver 2006).

Haultain (1971) reported that the Japanese frequently visited the coastal areas of *Gu-jingarliya* territory – flouting Australian law – and had entered the Blyth River at least four times to replenish water supplies (e.g. *Northern Standard* 1938).

Europeans before 1940

The Liverpool River was recorded by the surveyor Captain Philip Parker King in 1818 and the Blyth River by the navigator Francis Cadell in 1867. Over the next 40 years, several other people made some contact with the area, including prospector Edward Robinson (1875), explorer David Lindsay and surveyor Walter Cuthbertson (1883), explorer and surveyor Captain Carrington (1885), customs collector Alfred Searcy (1885), and Government Medical Officer Cecil Strangman (1908). In later times, crocodile hunters and pearl fishers visited the area between the Liverpool and Blyth Rivers (Hiatt 1965; Meehan 1982a, 17).

The Methodist Overseas Mission established outposts at Goulburn Island in 1916 and at Milingimbi in 1925 respectively (Hiatt 1965, 7). Apparently, Blyth River people visited Milingimbi to buy items from the trade store, but because they "were not on very good terms with the local people they usually left soon after". The Reverend T.T. Webb, stationed at Milingimbi prior to World War II, commented:

> One of the least known parts of Arnhem Land country is that along the Blyth River, which enters the sea in the southeast corner of Boucaut Bay about 30 miles from Milingimbi… The natives from this area are quite different stock from the majority of our station people… (Grant 1995; Meehan 1982a, 17).

In 1936–37, the anthropologist Donald Thomson visited Cape Stewart, at the request of the Australian government, to report on the conditions on the reserve (Meehan 1982a, 17; Peterson 2003). In 1939, mission employee Gordon Sweeney made a survey of the coast between the Blyth River and slightly west of the Liverpool River and found that "the ceremonial life and tribal authorities of groups between the two rivers were still intact". His report contains information about the settlement patterns, diet and ceremonial life of the people from that region prior to permanent European settlement. It also included a recommendation that people from the Goulburn Island Mission visit this area regularly to set up medical and "evangelical" bases (Sweeney 1939).

Europeans after 1940

World War II intervened, and the implementation of Sweeney's plans was delayed for 20 years. This delay may well have enabled Aboriginal people from this area (including the *An-barra*) to maintain their traditional culture until the present day and to return to their estate with confidence in the late 1960s. In 1955, Sweeney, then employed by the Welfare Branch, carried out a census in the Liverpool–Blyth River region. He contacted many *Gu-jingarliya* people who were camped at several sites where Betty and Rhys resided during 1972–73 (Hiatt 1965, 8–13; Meehan 1982a, 18–21).

The formal part of the settlement of Maningrida was set up by 1957 with the arrival of welfare workers David and Ingrid Drysdale and with the help of two patrol officers, Trevor Milikins and Ted Egan. Les Hiatt and Betty Meehan arrived on Curly Bell's boat in 1958. By 1970, Maningrida was the fifth-largest town in the NT (Meehan 1982a, 18–19).

Outstation movement

When the Woodward Commission recommended Aboriginal land rights in 1972, many Aboriginal groups began reoccupying their traditional homelands. This recommendation was not the only reason but was part of a general phenomenon in northern Australia at the time resulting from disenchantment with low living standards, overcrowding, friction between different language groups, and the resultant violence and symptoms of social breakdown. The *An-barra* were no exception, and they moved back to their land around the mouth of *An-gartcha Wana* (Meehan 1982a, 19–21; Meehan & Jones 1980). It was here that Betty and Rhys lived with them on and off throughout the 1970s.

Regional archaeological investigations

Prior to the commencement of the *An-barra* Archaeological Project in 1972–73, only a few studies had been undertaken in central Arnhem Land. Nearby at Milingimbi, 35 km east of the mouth of *An-gartcha Wana*, earth mounds, shell mounds and middens dating to the late Holocene have been recorded (Brockwell et al. 2009, 2011; McCarthy & Setzler 1960; Mulvaney 1975; Roberts 1994). Further east, Peterson (1973) recorded earth mounds around the Arafura Swamp. Brandl (1988) recorded rock art in shelters on the nearby Cadell River to the west.

In eastern Arnhem Land, shell middens and mounds, rock art and rock shelter sites and Macassan sites have been recorded at Blue Mud Bay (Faulkner 2013), on Groote Eylandt (Clarke & Frederick 2006; Frederick & Clarke 2011) and on Vanderlin Island (Oertle et al. 2014; Sim & Wallis 2008).

In western Arnhem Land, rock art and rock shelter sites, some dating back to the Pleistocene, have been recorded in the Wellington Range (May et al. 2010; Wesley et al. 2018; Wright et al. 2023) and the Arnhem Land escarpment (David et al. 2017), and shell middens and Macassan sites have been recorded on the Coburg Peninsula and Anuru Bay (Mitchell 1996; Wesley et al. 2016). In Kakadu, many Pleistocene and Holocene sites have been investigated, including rock shelters, rock art sites, shell mounds and middens, earth mounds and artefact concentrations, as well as Madjedbebe rock shelter, the oldest recorded site in Australia (e.g. Brockwell et al. 2020; Chaloupka 1993; Clarkson et al. 2017; Jones 1985a; Kamminga & Allen 1973; May et al. 2015; Ó Foghlú 2017; Schrire 1982; Shine et al. 2013; Taçon & Brockwell 1995).

The *An-barra* Archaeological Project

The *An-barra* Archaeological Project (Brockwell et al. 2005; Meehan 1995) investigated archaeological sites located in the vicinity of *An-gartcha Wana*. Most of these sites belong to the *An-barra* community; a few to other communities. The *An-barra* and other communities are part of the "Gidjingali who were divided into 19 groups each owning a cluster of sites and the surrounding countryside" (Hiatt 1965, 14, Maps 3–4, Table 1). The land owned by these communities stretches from the western side of the Blyth River to Cape Stewart in the east, approximately 20 km of coastline (Map 1.1). In 1875, on his way to the Gulf of Carpentaria, Edward Robinson encountered some Aboriginal people at Cape Stewart – the most eastern land accessed by *Gu-jingarliya* speakers. Of this encounter, Robinson said that Aboriginal people at Cape Stewart frightened his prospecting party (Hiatt 1965, 9). Betty Meehan and Rhys Jones walked from *Gupanga* to Cape Stewart to attend a ceremony with several *An-barra* people in 1973.

Betty and Rhys collected archaeological assemblages from these sites during numerous research trips over 40 years between 1972 and 2015, with the support of Traditional Owners Frank Gurrmanamana (deceased), his wife, Nancy Bandeiyama (deceased), their daughter Betty Ngurrpangurrpa, and other family and community members.

Prior to October 2002, the *An-barra* archaeological collection was housed in the ANU storage facility at its Weston campus in Canberra. Most of it was moved to ANU's main campus in Acton before the Canberra fire storm in January 2003, which destroyed 500 houses in the suburbs of Weston Creek, along with the ANU

Weston store. Two boxes of *An-barra* archaeological material were lost: *Muyu a-jirrapa* Shell Mound; and soil samples from *Ji-bena* mound (Swete Kelly & Phear 2004).

Initially, ANU's School of Archaeology and Anthropology in the College of Arts and Social Sciences provided storage facilities for the *An-barra* collection while the material was being sorted. In 2005, the collection was moved to the osteology laboratory in Archaeology and Natural History (ANH), School of Culture, History and Language, ANU College of Asia and the Pacific. Both departments provided office facilities for Sally Brockwell, who worked part-time on the *An-barra* Archaeological Project, funded by an AIATSIS grant from October 2002 until February 2004. Betty acted as honorary supervisor while Sally undertook the analysis and writing up (Brockwell et al. 2005). Both made a short field trip to Maningrida in August 2003, so Betty could renew contact with the *An-barra* community and Sally could meet them and see the archaeological sites in context. An additional visit associated with the project was made to Maningrida by Betty and Sally in 2015. Following completion of the analysis, the *An-barra* collection was repatriated to the Museum and Art Gallery of the Northern Territory (MAGNT) in Darwin in 2018.

Aim

The aim of the *An-barra* Archaeological Project (Brockwell et al. 2005; Meehan 1995) was to determine the nature of regional pre-colonial settlement patterns and subsistence strategies in central Arnhem Land against the backdrop of dramatic environmental change that took place on the coastal plains of northern Australia in the mid to late Holocene. The archaeological data was also compared with the ethnographic data presented in Betty's book *Shell Bed to Shell Midden* (Meehan 1982a), noting similarities and differences and seeking explanations. This current monograph details the results of the investigations and argues that the ethnographic data are relevant for interpretation of archaeological sites belonging to the recent past.

The *An-barra* archaeological sites consist of earth mounds, shell mounds, linear shell middens and transect material, containing shell, other faunal remains and a small amount of stone. See Chapter 2 for definitions of these different types of sites. Occupation dates from at least 3,500 years ago, but most of the sites are less than 1,000 years old (see Chronology in Chapter 2). This reflects late Holocene sedimentary infill and progradation of the coastal plains and the recent nature of their occupation (see below). The initial results of the *An-barra* Archaeological Project were compared with those of other studies in the Northern Territory to develop a model of regional use of the northern coastal plains in the late Holocene (see Brockwell et al. 2005, 2009, 2011, 2013).

During her time living and working with the *An-barra*, Betty made a distinction between "dead men" sites and "Dreaming" sites (1982a, 166–8; see also Brockwell 2013). "Dead men" sites are those that the *An-barra* recognise as being made and used by their ancestors, such as shell middens. "Dreaming" sites are those they believe were created by supernatural beings in the Dreamtime, such as the large shell mounds. As Betty went on to say, "the fascinating problems raised by these data point to a logical direction for subsequent research… Only an archaeological study of the Blyth River region can ultimately place the year I spent among the *Anbarra* in its proper context" (Meehan 1982a, 168). This theme is explored in this monograph.

Significance

The *An-barra* archaeological collection is the only one of its kind from coastal central Arnhem Land. It documents the settlement patterns and economic strategies of the *An-barra* people of *An-gartcha Wana* over the last 3,500 years. It shows how the *An-barra* occupied new sites in their territory as the coast prograded to the north in the late Holocene. Comparisons between ethnographic shell-fishing strategies (Meehan 1982a) and the contents of the middens demonstrate change over time most likely associated with climate and environmental change. Some aspects of the archaeological analysis have been published previously (see Bourke et al. 2007; Brockwell 2013; Brockwell et al. 2005, 2009, 2011, 2013; Meehan 1982a). However, this monograph contains the results of a more complete analysis. The archaeological collection is companion to the *An-gartcha Wana* ethnographic collection donated to MAGNT by Betty in 2005. Together these collections offer potential for further study and insights into the ethnography and archaeology of an Aboriginal community in central Arnhem Land in the late Holocene.

2
STUDY AREA AND METHODOLOGY

Location

An-gartcha Wana is located on the coastal plains of northern Australia, 12 degrees south of the Equator in a subtropical savanna environment, in the "Top End" of the NT. The river rises in the Arnhem Land plateau to the south and flows into Boucaut Bay in the Arafura Sea. The study area is located 40 km east of the township of Maningrida in central Arnhem Land. It is bounded by the Arnhem Land escarpment to the south, the Arafura Sea to the north, the Liverpool River to the west and Cape Stewart to the east (Map 1.1, Figure 2.1; Meehan 1982a, 10–11).

Climate and landscape change during the mid to late Holocene

As in other parts of the northern coastal plains, following the Last Glacial Maximum, down-cut river valleys of Arnhem Land were drowned during post-Pleistocene sea-level rise, which flooded the Torres Strait and cut off New Guinea from Australia c. 12,000 years ago (Williams et al. 2018). Although there are common elements, the environmental histories of each region in the Top End are governed by catchment size, tides, sediments and local features of the topography, which can differ considerably, affecting aspects of the cultural landscape (Brockwell 2001).

A warmer and wetter period occurred between about 9,000 to 6,000 years BP (Reeves et al. 2013; Rowe et al. 2019; Williams et al. 2015). During this time, processes of sedimentation following sea-level stabilisation in the mid Holocene formed vast mangrove swamps in the estuarine systems of the Top End, including *An-gartcha Wana*, from about 7,000 to 4,000 years BP, the "Big Swamp" Phase (Chappell 1988, 2001; Chappell & Woodroffe 1985; Hope et al. 1985; Woodroffe 1988; Woodroffe et al. 1985).

Figure 2.1. Aerial view of *An-gartcha Wana.*

Northern Australia appears to have become drier during the mid to late Holocene, with studies drawing a possible link to the emergence of enhanced El Niño Southern Oscillation (ENSO) conditions between c. 5,000–2,000 years BP (McGowan et al. 2012; Williams et al. 2015). The mid to late Holocene was punctuated by millennial-scale variability, associated with ENSO, which is evident in the marine, coral, speleothem and pollen records of the region (Reeves et al. 2013; Rowe et al. 2019; Stevenson et al. 2015).

This drier period in northern Australia led to the formation of chenier ridges, elongated deposits made up of sand and shell, on mudflats and saline tidal flats, which initiated chenier-building and coastal progradation (Clark & Guppy 1988;

Mulrennan & Woodroffe 1998; O'Connor & Sullivan 1994; Woodroffe et al. 1985). In the Top End, siltation and coastal progradation reduced the extent of tidal influence and the mangroves retreated towards the coast and the edges of waterways, and saline mudflats were formed. As high-tide flooding became rarer, brackish and freshwater swamps formed in residual depressions on the landward edge of the coastal plains. This "Transition" Phase occurred between 5,000 and 2,000 years BP, depending on the river system (Chappell 1988, 2001; Clark & Guppy 1988; Hope et al. 1985), and coincides with the onset of ENSO.

Climate amelioration was brought about by more pervasive La Niña conditions post-2,000 years BP (Williams et al. 2015). Freshwater from monsoon rains ponded behind the cheniers, and freshwater wetlands became widespread after 2,000 years on the floodplains of the Top End. This is called the "Freshwater" Phase (Chappell 1988; Clark and Guppy 1988; Hope et al. 1985; Mulrennan and Woodroffe 1998; Woodroffe 1988).

Geomorphology on the floodplains of *An-gartcha Wana*

John Chappell and Rhys Jones (1999) undertook geomorphological fieldwork to obtain core samples in collaboration with the *An-barra* community, especially Betty Ngurrpangurrpa and Ranger Stewart Rankin. This work, along with the radiocarbon dates from the geomorphological research, has enabled the archaeological data to be linked to the background environmental data and chronology concerning the evolutionary sequence common to the floodplains of northern Australia in the mid to late Holocene.

The following information is based on their field notes. Dating samples were taken from cores at eight locations from the coast to *Balpilja* Swamp. The geomorphological sites are, from the sea inland:

1. *Jinawunya*
2. *Gulukula*
3. *Lorrkon a-jirrapa*
4. *An-mal Mandayerra*
5. *Ngalpura Jinyu-nirripa* 2
6. *Ngalpura Jinyu-nirripa* 3
7. *Ji-bena*
8. *Anamanba*

Several of these sites have the same location as the archaeological sites described in the next chapter (Map 2.1). Due to coastal progradation in the late Holocene, the closer to the coast, the younger the dates (Tables 2.1 and 2.2). A limitation

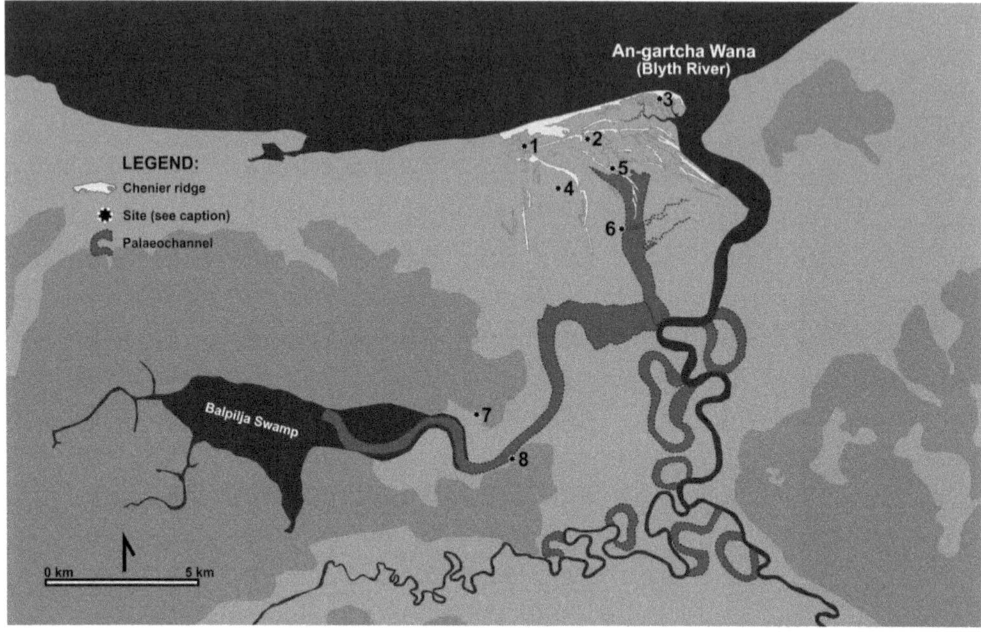

Map 2.1. Geomorphological sample sites: 1. *Jinawunya*; 2. *Gulukula*; 3. *Lorrkon a-jirrapa*; 4. *An-mal Mandayerra*; 5. *Ngalpura Jinyu-nirripa* 2; 6. *Ngalpura Jinyu-nirripa* 3; 7. *Ji-bena*; 8. *Anamanba* (Billy Ó Foghlú).

of these data is that we cannot establish from Jones and Chappell's notes whether some of the geomorphological dating samples were on shell or charcoal. Nor did they record which radiocarbon laboratory did the dating. Therefore, three of the radiocarbon dates from two sample sites (*Ngalpura Jinyu-nirripa* 2 and 3) were calibrated with OxCal (Bronk Ramsey 2024) using both the Marine20 (Heaton et al. 2020) and the SHCal20 calibration curve (Hogg et al. 2020). The local marine ΔR has been determined via Ulm et al. (2023) using approximate site coordinates (decimal latitude/longitude).

Balpilja Swamp was previously an ancient valley drowned during early Holocene sea-level rise. Chappell predicted that the formation beneath the swamp dates to the late Pleistocene. He estimated that the eastern part of *Balpilja* formed a palaeo-estuary some 6,000–7,000 years ago. Today, *Balpilja* is a freshwater swamp lying 8 km from the coast, indicating the extent of coastal progradation over the mid to late Holocene.

The *Ngalpura Jinyu-nirripa* chenier ridge lies approximately 3 km inland from the coast (Map 2.1). The core at *Ngalpura Jinyu-nirripa* 3 was taken from under the ridge at 2.5 m and is the oldest dated geomorphological site on the *An-gartcha Wana* floodplains. The blue, grey mangrove mud from the sample dates the Big Swamp Phase here from 9,291–7,880 cal BP (Blyth 1399).

Table 2.1. *An-gartcha Wana* geomorphology dates.

Site (no. Map 2.1)	Lab. Code	Age C^{14}	Local Marine ΔR	Cal. Curve	Age cal BP 2σ	Cal. Curve	Age cal BP 2σ
Big Swamp Phase							
Ngalpura Jinyu-nirripa 3 (6)	Blyth 1399	7890±210	-141±36	Marine 20	8922–7880	SHCal 20	9291–8209
Anamanba (8)	Blyth 1599	5656±202	-141±36	-	-	SHCal 20	6891–5940
Ji-bena 1999 (7)	Blyth 1199	4980±170	-141±36	-	-	SHCal 20	6175–5312
Ngalpura Jinyu-nirripa 3 (6)	Blyth 1299	3970±90	-141±36	Marine 20	4287–3681	SHCal 20	4795–4090
Transition/Chenier-Building Phase							
An-mal Mandayerra (4)	Blyth 799	3840±220	-140±36	-	-	SHCal 20	4833–3639
Ngalpura Jinyu-nirripa 2 (5)	Blyth 899	2510±210	-141±36	Marine 20	2728–1661	SHCal 20	3058–2010
Freshwater/Chenier-Building Phase							
Lorrkon a-jirrapa 1999 (3)	Blyth 399	2040±80	-141±36	Marine 20	1839–1355	-	-
Jinawunya 1999 (1)	ANU-11207	1530±60	-140±36	Marine 20	1264–887	-	-
Gulukula 1999 (2)	Blyth 199	1420±60	-140±36	Marine 20	1150–750	-	-

Calibrations performed via OxCal 4.4.4 [173] (Bronk Ramsey 2009, 2024) using Marine20 (Heaton et al. 2020) or SHCal 20 (Hogg et al. 2020). The local marine ΔR has been determined via Ulm et al. (2023) using approximate site coordinates (decimal lat/long).

Table 2.2. *An-gartcha Wana* geomorphology phases.

Site (no. Map 2.1)	Lab. Code	Substrate	Sample	Location	Depth (cm)
Big Swamp Phase					
Ngalpura Jinyu-nirripa 3 (6)	Blyth 1399	Blue, grey mangrove mud, sparse organics & broken shell	?	End of ridge	250
Anamanba (8)	Blyth 1599	Black swamp clay, over red-mottled clay, over light grey clay with organics	Charcoal	*Eleocharis* swamp at margin of *Balpilja* palaeochannel	30–80
Ji-bena 1999 (7)	Blyth 1199	Dark grey mangrove mud with organics	Charcoal	Palaeochannel	240
Ngalpura Jinyu-nirripa 3 (6)	Blyth 1299	Blue, grey mangrove mud, sparse organics & broken shell	?	End of ridge	180
Transition/Chenier-Building Phase					
An-mal Mandayerra (4)	Blyth 799	Clay with organics	Charcoal	Under ridge	270
Ngalpura Jinyu-nirripa 2 (5)	Blyth 899	Yellow, mottled grey clay	?	Under ridge	150
Freshwater/Chenier-Building Phase					
Lorrkon a-jirrapa 1999 (3)	Blyth 399	Shelly sand	Shell	Chenier base	240–250
Jinawunya 1999 (1)	ANU-11207	Grey mud	*Dosinia juvenilis*	Next to well	40
Gulukula 1999 (2)	Blyth 199	Shelly sand	Shell	Chenier next to shell mound	145

At *Anamanba*, next to the archaeological site of the same name described in the following chapter, light grey clay with organics taken from an *Eleocharis* swamp next to *Balpilja* palaeochannel were dated to 6,891–5,940 cal BP (Blyth 1599). In the palaeochannel next to *Ji-bena*, where the archaeological site is also located, the Big Swamp Phase was dated to 6,175–5,312 cal BP (Blyth 1199). Mangrove mud from another sample taken at 180 cm from *Ngalpura Jinyu-nirripa* 3 shows that the Big Swamp Phase persisted at least until 4,795 cal BP (Blyth 1299) on the *An-gartcha Wana* floodplains (Table 2.2). During this period, the coast was further inland and the *Balpilja* palaeo-estuary was active until c. 6,000–7,000 years BP (Map 2.1).

During the following Transition Phase, the drier climate initiated chenier-building and coastal progradation was pronounced in the region. At *An-mal Mandayerra*, this phase was dated to 4,833–3,639 cal BP (Blyth 799) from a sample 2.7 m below the surface. This phase persisted until at least 3,058–1,661 cal BP (Blyth 899), based on a sample taken at 1.5 m at *Ngalpura Jinyu-nirripa* 2 (Map 2.1, Table 2.2). The radiocarbon chronology shows that the coastline advanced rapidly seaward at up to 50 m per century in the last 2,000 years (Chappell & Jones 1999, 93). The near-coastal cheniers are all less than 2,000 years old and track the advancing coastline. The sample from the base of *Lorrkon a-jirrapa* chenier 3 km inland, next to the archaeological site of the same name, dates to 1,839–1,355 cal BP (Blyth 399) (Map 2.1, Table 2.2). The *Gulukula* chenier, next to the shell mounds of the same name, lies approximately 1 km inland. A sample taken from 1.45 m dates from 1,150–750 cal BP (Blyth 199). The *Jinawunya* chenier, which is associated with the archaeological site, is closest to the coast and was dated 1,264–887 cal BP (ANU-11207). The coastline continued to prograde, as Betty noted from comparing aerial photographs of the Blyth River mouth in 1958 and 1968 (Meehan 1982a, 15).

With increasing rainfall and sedimentation in the last 2,000 years, large mangrove swamps behind the cheniers became freshwater wetlands. It was during this Freshwater Phase that *Balpilja* Swamp next to *Ji-bena* mound became freshwater (Table 2.2; Brockwell 2013; Chappell & Jones 1999; Thurtell et al. 1999). The geomorphological evidence and dates show that the evolution of the *An-gartcha Wana* landscape is recent and conforms with that of other river systems of the Top End. The alluvial and coastal systems are still actively changing (Thurtell et al. 1999, 8). The *An-barra* are keenly aware of their mobile landscape with dune build-up, storm erosion, shifting mangroves and river channels. These memories are preserved in their mythology, and they treat such changing areas with respect in the hopes they will remain stable (Meehan 1982a, 15–16).

Climate and landscape today

Today, the coastal plains of northern Australia lie within the dry tropics. The climate is markedly seasonal with a long dry season, dominated by southeast trade winds, lasting roughly from May to November, and a shorter wet season from December to April, dominated by the northwest monsoon (Christian & Stewart 1953, 29). This cycle is reliable from year to year in the Top End, a feature that distinguishes it from regions further to the south where it can be unreliable (McDonald & McAlpine 1991, 19). Rainfall is high in the wet season with an average of 1,291 mm per annum at Maningrida, most of which occurs between December and March (Thurtell et al. 1999, 9). The average daytime temperatures remain stable throughout the year, ranging from 30.1°C in July to 33.4°C in November. More significant in terms of human comfort are the variations in night-time temperatures, averaging from 17.2°C in July to 25.1°C in December, and the relative humidity, which builds up from September and remains high throughout the wet season (Bureau of Meteorology 2024). The most stressful time of year is the late dry season, October through December, when both day and night-time temperatures are high, and the humidity builds up often without the relief of rain.

The hydrology of the coastal plains of northern Australia is regulated by its strongly monsoonal climate. The groundwater builds up in the wet season and maximum run-off occurs late in the season (Chappell & Woodroffe 1985, 90). Floodplain areas are inundated during the wet season making many places accessible only by watercraft. These areas dry out progressively through the dry season. By the late dry season most of the floodplains have dried out, except for low-lying areas which remain submerged for most or all the year.

The land owned by the *An-barra* has been described in detail by Meehan (1982a). In brief, after *An-gartcha Wana* leaves the escarpment, it flows across savanna plains through dry *Eucalyptus tetradonta* woodland. Within 40 km of its mouth, it joins the Cadell River and becomes tidal and brackish. The coast is a soft shore with sandy mudflats and little or no offshore reefs. This environment limits the diversity of shellfish species available. The land surrounding this area supports a mosaic of productive habitats, including freshwater wetlands, mangroves, monsoon rainforest and pandanus groves (Map 2.2; Meehan 1982a, 10–12).

Within this rich environment of sea, estuary and freshwater wetlands, there are abundant seasonal food resources available to the *An-barra*, including shellfish, fish, crabs, stingrays, turtles, reptiles (including crocodiles), buffalo, wallaby, birds (especially geese), a great variety of fruits and vegetables, and small delicacies such as honey and mangrove worms. Most of these items were eaten by the *An-barra* while Rhys and Betty were living with them on their own land and have been previously

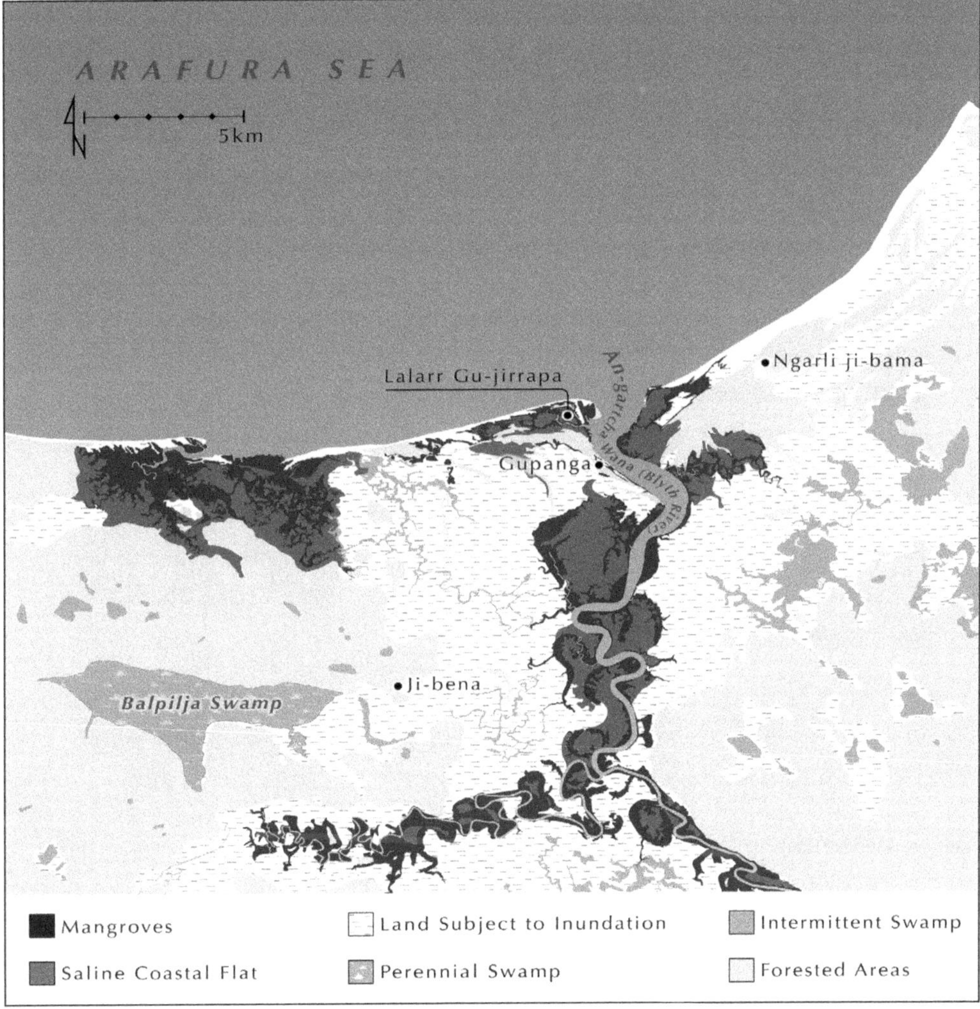

Map 2.2. Environmental zones (Adam Black).

described in detail (Jones 1980; Jones & Meehan 1989; Meehan 1982a, 1982b). Shellfish are particularly relevant to archaeology as shells are the most likely remains to survive in archaeological sites (see Appendix 2 for a list of shellfish species and their habitats). While Rhys and Betty lived with them in the 1970s, the *An-barra* also had access to European food, mainly tea, sugar and flour.

Methodology

Archaeological fieldwork

Most of the fieldwork for the *An-barra* Archaeological Project was undertaken by Betty Meehan and Rhys Jones between 1972 and 1980, as detailed in Betty's book

Shell Bed to Shell Midden (Meehan 1982a, 162–8). There are three main types of archaeological sites: shell middens, shell mounds and earth mounds (*gun-gapula*).

Shell middens

A shell midden has been defined as "an archaeological deposit consisting primarily of mollusc shells resulting from food procurement activities" (Bahn 1992, 453). Bourke (2012, 28) elaborates on middens in the Darwin region:

> Shell middens…are deposits containing more than (an estimated) 50% by weight of shells, occurring somewhere in the open, near a beach or estuary or rocky shoreline, or an inland lake or river. These shells have been deposited by humans exploiting marine, estuarine and riverine resources. Middens may take the form of a thin layer of shell over, or just below (subsurface), the land surface, or a thick mound of shell… [They] are usually circular, but may also be elongated or irregular in shape, or doughnut-shaped (shell rings) around a central area containing little or no shell. Unstratified surface scatters of shell also occur.

Meehan (1982a, 166) describes shell middens as "one of the common features of *An-barra* territory, both inland and on the coast, and they occur in many forms ranging from thin scatters to dense layers of shell up to one metre thick".

Shell mounds

Meehan (1982a, 167) describes shell mounds in *An-barra* country as "[l]arge discrete mounds of shells measuring anything up to 5 m in height to 30 m in diameter [that] are dramatic features of the Blyth River landscape. The mounds do not occur on the coast but inland at least 1 km on a series of fossil dunes. They are found on both sides of the river in *Anbarra*, *Gulala* and *Matai* territory."

Earth mounds

Brockwell (2006, 47) defines earth mounds as "sites that are composed mostly of soil and sand. Depending on their location, they may also contain stone artefacts and faunal remains, including shell."

Field trips to Maningrida in the 2000s

In the 2000s, Betty and Sally travelled to Maningrida twice. The aim of the first trip, from 4–7 August 2003 and funded by AIATSIS, was to introduce Sally to members of the *An-barra* Aboriginal community. Sally had already met Betty Ngurrpangurrpa when she came to Canberra for the launch of the book and CD, *People of the Rivermouth* (Gurrmanamana et al. 2002), but it was important that other members of that community were able to meet and talk with her as well. We stayed in the Maningrida Progress Association's motel. Many *An-barra* people now reside more or less permanently in Maningrida, so Sally was able to meet many of them there. Many of these people were children when Betty and Rhys carried out work at the *An-gartcha Wana* during the 1970s. Most of them now have their own households and many children. While at Maningrida, we were also able to visit the graves of recently deceased *An-barra* people, most significantly those of Frank Gurrmanamana and his daughter Nancy Djinbor, both of whom died in 2003.

Eventually, we were able to hire a four-wheel drive vehicle so that we could visit *Gupanga* and *Ji-bena* where Sally visited the sites Betty and Rhys excavated in 1978 and 1979. Two sites, adjacent to *Gupanga* on the western bank of the *An-gartcha Wana*, *Muyu a-jirrapa* linear midden and *Muyu a-jirrapa* mound, unfortunately no longer exist. They have been eroded away by the wet season flooding of *An-gartcha Wana*. However, Sally was able to inspect the surrounding environment to get some idea of the physical context of these important sites. *Ji-bena* mound is situated some 8 km from the coast on the banks of the freshwater *Balpilja* Swamp and remains in good condition. While at *Ji-bena*, we were also able to visit the grave of Nancy Bandeiyama with whom Betty had worked since 1958.

More recently, we visited Maningrida from 10–14 August 2015, this time accompanied by ANU doctoral student Bethune Carmichael who was conducting fieldwork with rangers from the *Djelk* Indigenous Protected Area. Betty Ngurrpangurrpa and her husband, Dominic Mason, again guided us on their land. We visited the *Gulukula* shell mounds and the coastal site of *Jinawunya* (Figure 2.2). Betty Ngurrpangurrpa was interviewed by Bethune Carmichael (2015) for his video, *Places in Peril – Archaeology in the Anthropocene*, in which she described the destruction of the coastal midden at *Jinawunya* by wave action. With Betty's and Dominic's permission, we took a shell sample to date this site (see Chronology next chapter). We also collected from the beach a selection of shellfish species that are eaten by the *An-barra* today and in the recent past. These species also occur in the archaeological assemblages. They will be used for stable isotope analysis to examine potential changes in sea surface temperature in the late Holocene, a study being undertaken by Dr Mirani Litster and Dr Ian Moffat (Flinders University). Our discussions with Betty Ngurrpangurrpa indicated that she and other members of her community are pleased that we are working on these sites and look forward to receiving the results.

Darwin

In Darwin, also in 2015, we were able to talk to various people about our work and obtain relevant comparative material. We met with Dr Patricia Bourke from

Figure 2.2. Maningrida visit 2015 (Bethune Carmichael).

the Centre for Indigenous Natural and Cultural Resource Management at Charles Darwin University. She has carried out extensive archaeological work on shell mounds in the Darwin region (Bourke 2012) and the results of her project are relevant to our research at *An-gartcha Wana*. We also held discussions with Dr Christine Tarbett-Buckley (former Head of Collections at the MAGNT) about the possibility of placing archaeological material from our project with that institution when our analysis was complete. Betty had been negotiating with Dr Tarbett-Buckley for some time about donating a collection of *An-barra* material culture that she and Rhys accumulated during their fieldwork in the 1970s, which was eventually donated to MAGNT in 2015. It seemed appropriate that the archaeological material should be housed in the same place. In 2018, Betty and Sally repatriated the *An-barra* archaeological collection to MAGNT.

Excavations and laboratory analysis

The sampling and excavation methods employed by Betty and Rhys at each site are detailed in the following chapter under the site descriptions. Sometimes, the deposit was sieved on site; other times, a solid sample was taken. In the latter case, this sample was weighed and sieved at ANU through 1.5 mm mesh and its contents analysed.

As field bucket weights for the deposit from excavations were not recorded, the weight of deposit has been estimated at 1,500 kg per cubic metre (Jones & Johnson 1985, 183). On this basis, we were able to calculate the minimum number of individuals (MNI) of shells per kg of deposit, so that results from each spit could be compared over time. In other cases, where the size and weight of a sample is unknown, just the MNI of the shellfish species is listed.

Most of the assemblages consisted of shell, both marine and estuarine. In the field, shellfish were originally identified by the *An-barra* themselves (Appendix 2). For her PhD analysis, Betty had shellfish identified by Dr Philip Colman and Dr Winston Ponder of the Australian Museum (Meehan 1982a, ix). Rhys and Freda Stewart (Department of Prehistory, Research School of Pacific Studies, ANU) did some initial MNI analysis of shell assemblages, and these counts were published by Meehan (1982a, 166–8). Later identifications were undertaken at ANU by Sally and Dr Ella Ussher. They used the shellfish reference collection in ANH, Betty's own identified specimens from *An-gartcha Wana*, and identifications by Dr Richard Willan.

Identification was not attempted on shell fragments less than 3 mm. Unidentified fragments were bagged, weighed and labelled "Unidentified Shell". MNI, NISP (number of identified specimens) and weight were calculated for identified specimens. MNI was estimated mostly by the spire in gastropods, e.g. *Telescopium* and *Terebralia*, and the umbo or hinge in bivalves, e.g. *Geloina*, *Marcia* and *Tegillarca* (Bourke 2012; Claassen 1998). The molluscan taxa were mostly identified to genus level, but in some cases to species level, e.g. *Dosinia juvenilis*.

Other faunal material (mainly turtle and fish) and stone artefacts were present in some sites. Fish and turtle were identified by Sally Brockwell to species level where possible using the comparative faunal collections in ANH and MAGNT. Humanly introduced stone was classified according to raw materials (mainly chert and quartzite) and degrees of modification. All data were recorded on laboratory forms and entered onto an Access database, designed specifically for this kind of analysis, and processed in Excel.

The results of the analysis are detailed in the following chapter. All these assemblages are stored at MAGNT and are available for future, more detailed analysis, such as species richness, representativeness, taxonomic evenness, taxonomic heterogeneity and more comprehensive MNI analysis (Faulkner et al. 2021; Harris et al. 2015; Ortiz-Burgos 2016).

Presentation of results

The latter part of the project consisted of writing up results for publication and producing a community report. The extensive field journals of Betty and Rhys and their many publications on the area (e.g. Fullagar et al. 1999; Jones 1980, 1983, 1985b; Jones & Bowler 1980; Jones & Meehan 1989; Meehan 1982a, 1982b, 1983, 1988a, 1988b, 1991, 1995; Meehan & Jones 1980, 1986, 2005; Meehan et al. 1979, 1999) were used to establish the background of the research. Throughout the project, Betty has provided information regarding the social context. She has also provided most of the photographs used in the publication.

Initial outcomes from the *An-barra* Archaeological Project were presented in several ways. Betty published preliminary findings in 1995 (Meehan 1995). Betty and Sally gave a paper on the archaeology of the *Ji-bena* mound and the geomorphology of *An-gartcha Wana* at the Australian Archaeological Association (AAA) conference in Jindabyne in 2003. A research report detailing the findings of the archaeological analysis was published in the AIATSIS journal *Australian Aboriginal Studies* (Brockwell et al. 2005). Sally presented a paper on the dating of the archaeological sites at the AAA conference in Beechworth in 2006, along with Dr Patricia Bourke (CDU), and at AAA in Adelaide in 2009. The results of these studies were published in two papers on the Holocene settlement of the NT coastal plains (Brockwell et al. 2011, 2013). Sally also published a paper on the *An-barra* archaeological sites and ethnographic analogy (Brockwell 2013). Chapter 5 contains a plain language report for the *An-barra* community in English and *Gu-jingarliya.*

3

ARCHAEOLOGICAL SITES

This chapter contains the archaeological site reports, including excavation and sampling methods, chronology, and the results of the analyses, for:

- *Agajang-guwa*
- *Anamanba*
- *Aningarra's* Camp 1974
- *Gulukula* Mounds 1974, 1978
- *Guna-jengga* 1974
- *Gupanga wangarr an-dakal a-yurra*
- *Ji-bena* 1978, 1979
- *Jilangga a-jirra*
- *Jinawunya* 1978
- *Jurnaka* 1978
- *Lorrkon a-jirrapa* East 1974
- *Lorrkon a-jirrapa* West 1974, 1978
- *Mu-garnbal* 1973
- *Muyu a-jirrapa* Coastal Shell Midden 1974, 1978
- *Muyu a-jirrapa* Shell Mound 1974, 1978
- *Ngarli ji-bama* 1974
- *Yuluk a-jirrapa* Mounds 1974 (Map 3.1).

Site descriptions come from *Shell Bed to Shell Midden* (Meehan 1982a), the field notes of Betty Meehan (BM) and Rhys Jones (RJ), and the radiocarbon submission sheets. *Gupanga*, *Lalarr gu-jirrapa* and *Ngarli ji-bama* were home bases for the *An-barra* when Betty and Rhys did their fieldwork in 1972–73 (Figure 2.1, Map 2.2; Meehan 1982a, 26–9).

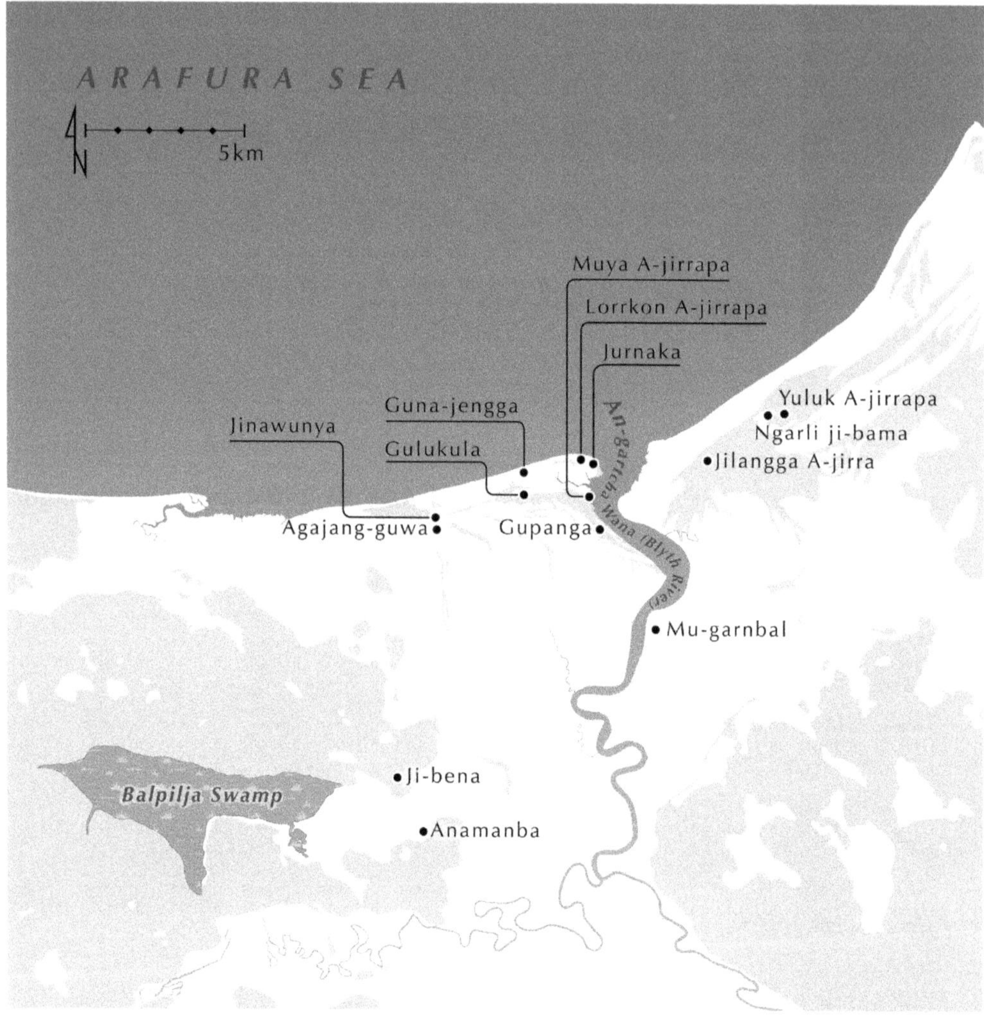

Map 3.1. Archaeological sites (Adam Black).

Chronology

Not all sites recorded by Betty and Rhys were selected for dating and analysis. The original dating of the excavation and sampling program undertaken in the 1970s was done by the ANU Radiocarbon Laboratory. In the 2000s, the Centre for Archaeological Research at ANU (CAR) provided funding for radiocarbon dates. Samples (shell and charcoal) were sent to the ANU Radiocarbon Laboratory and to the Waikato Radiocarbon Dating Laboratory in New Zealand. The results are listed in Table 3.1. Further dating and analysis of more sites is possible in the future, as there are suitable samples of charcoal and shell available, stored at MAGNT in Darwin.

Agajang-guwa

Site description

Agajang-guwa is an area just south of *Jinawunya* where there is a shell midden on a transverse dune chenier running east–west.

Sampling

Rhys took a *Dosinia juvenilis* sample from the lower level of the midden in 1978.

Chronology

The sample returned a date of 1,060–683 cal BP (ANU-11209) (Table 3.1).

Anamanba

Site description

Anamanba lies on the eastern side of *Balpilja* Swamp (Maps 2.1 and 3.1). There is a large earth mound composed of termite nest and some shell lenses. This mound, like many others in the area including *Ji-bena* (see below), is on the bank of a freshwater billabong.

Sampling

Anamanba mound was augured by Jones and Chappell in 1999. Shell samples were collected from 2.3 m below the surface of the mound.

Chronology

A sample of *Geloina coaxans* (ANU-11208) returned a date of 796–423 cal BP (Table 3.1).

Aningarra's Camp 1974

Site description

Michael *Aningarra* and his family camped on this shell midden, which sits on a coastal sand dune at *Gupanga* – a contemporary home base on the west bank near the mouth of *An-gartcha Wana* (Figure 2.1, Map 3.1). The upper levels of the midden were still occupied in 1974.

> The beach berm on the north side of Kopanga has been eroded by the tide, exposing thick, tightly packed layers of shell midden that can be traced intermittently along the entire beach front, the present-day occupation adding

Table 3.1. Dates for *An-gartcha Wana* archaeological sites.

Site	Type	Sample	Code	Age C^{14}	Local Marine ΔR	Calibration Curve	Age cal BP 2σ
Mu-garnbal	Midden	*Tegillarca granosa*	Wk-17746	3625±40	-141±36	Marine 20	3724–3345
Gupanga wangarr an-dakal a-yurra	Shell bed	*D. juvenilis*	ANU-2024	1890±90	-141±36	Marine 20	1695–1214
Lorrkon a-jirrapa 1999	Midden	Shell	Blyth 499	1710±60	-141±36	Marine 20	1433–1046
Lorrkon a-jirrapa 1999	Midden	Shell	Blyth 599	1460±80	-141±36	Marine 20	1228–772
Lorrkon a-jirrapa West 1974	Midden	*D. juvenilis*	ANU-2012	1440±70	-141±36	Marine 20	1179–750
Lorrkon a-jirrapa West 1974	Midden	Charcoal	ANU-2012	1190±155	-	SHCal 20	1345–740
Lorrkon a-jirrapa West 1978	Midden	*Dosinia* sp.	Wk-24233	1460±36	-141±36	Marine 20	1166–821
Muyu a-jirrapa	Shell midden	*D. juvenilis*	ANU-2014	1670±70	-141±36	Marine 20	1392–987
Muyu a-jirrapa	Shell mound	*D. juvenilis*	ANU-2816	1580±100	-141±36	Marine 20	1356–867
Jilangga a-jirra	Midden	*D. juvenilis*	ANU-2022	1430±110	-140±36	Marine 20	1235–703
Jilangga a-jirra	Midden	Charcoal	ANU-2022	270±60	-	SHCal 20	452–0*
Ji-bena 1/14	Earth mound	*D. juvenilis*	ANU-2817	1510±100	-141±36	Marine 20	1284–790
Ji-bena 1/13	Earth mound	*D. juvenilis*	ANU-3417	1360±70	-141±36	Marine 20	1088–680
Ji-bena 1 Auger/8-9	Earth mound	*D. juvenilis*	ANU-3414	1250±80	-141±36	Marine 20	985–573
Ji-bena 1/8	Earth mound	*D. juvenilis*	ANU-3416	1260±70	-141±36	Marine 20	988–609
Ji-bena 1/5	Earth mound	*D. juvenilis*	ANU-3415	970±80	-141±36	Marine 20	710–333

Site	Type	Sample	Code	Age C^{14}	Local Marine ΔR	Calibration Curve	Age cal BP 2σ
Agajang-guwa	Midden	*D. juvenilis*	ANU-11209	1350±60	-140±36	Marine 20	1060–683
Gulukula 1974	Shell mound	*D. juvenilis*	ANU-2021	1100±90	-140±36	Marine 20	875–465
Gulukula 1978	Shell mound	*Dosinia* sp.	Wk-24232	962±39	-140±36	Marine 20	666–392
Gulukula 1999	Shell mound	*Dosinia* sp.	Blyth 299	910±60	-140±36	Marine 20	641–312
Anamanba	Earth mound	*Geloina coaxans*	ANU-11208	1050±80	-141±36	Marine 20	796–423
Jinawunya 1983	Midden	*Dosinia* sp.	ANU-11206	1030±60	-140±36	Marine 20	740–430
Jinawunya 2015	Midden	*Anadara antiquata*	Wk-42262	454±30	140±36	Marine 20	40–0*
Yuluk a-jirrapa	Shell mound	*D. juvenilis*	ANU-2023	830±105	-140±36	Marine 20	636–165*
Yuluk a-jirrapa	Shell mound	Charcoal	ANU-2023	131.7±3.4	-	SHCal 20	240–23*
Aningarra's Camp	Midden	*D. juvenilis*	ANU-2013	740±70	-141±36	Marine 20	515–130*
Aningarra's Camp	Midden	Charcoal	ANU-2013	310±130	-	SHCal 20	505–0
Guna-jengga	Midden	Charcoal	ANU-2020	290±105	-	SHCal 20	495–0*
Guna-jengga	Midden	*D. juvenilis*	ANU-2020	600±105	-140±36	Marine 20	417–0*
Jurnaka	Midden	*Dosinia* sp.	Wk-24234	610±30	-141±36	Marine 20	373–14*
Ngarli ji-bama	Midden	*Mactra abbreviata*	Wk-17747	555±34	-140±36	Marine 20	286–0*

Calibrations performed via OxCal 4.4.4 [173] (Bronk Ramsey 2009, 2024) using Marine20 (Heaton et al. 2020) or SHCal 20 (Hogg et al. 2020). The local marine ΔR has been determined via Ulm et al. (2023) using approximate site coordinates (decimal lat/long). * "Date may extend out of range".

Table 3.2. *Aningarra*'s Camp Shellfish taxa (MNI).

		Marine								Mangrove					
		Dosinia	*Marcia*	*Mactra*	*Modiolus*	*Volegalea*	*Tegillarca*	*Placamen*		*Cerithidea*	*Crassostrea*	*Geloina*	*Telescopium*	*Cassidula*	
XU	**Depth (cm)**								**Total**						**Total**
UL	**0–6**	62	14	5	5	5	2	1	**94**	5	3	2	1	0	**11**
LL	**20–25**	57	26	8	5	3	4	1	**104**	1	2	0	0	1	**4**

> daily to the deposit. [Michael] Aningarra's [1972] camp was placed directly on a dense exposure of shell midden, one of his house posts being dug 30 cm into the deposit, which is almost 1 m thick at this point (Meehan 1982a,166).

> This feature measures approximately 8 yds by 5 yds with a 5-yard diameter of hard packed shell, charcoal etc. The excavation revealed 3 distinct layers overlaying sand (RJ 1974 FN Bk 1, 67–8).

Excavation

In 1974, after clearing the surface, Betty and Rhys excavated a 50 × 50 cm square down to sterile sand and took two solid samples: Upper Level (0–6 cm), Lower Level (20–25 cm). The midden itself was very dense and contained much fine charcoal and ash with many shells that were burnt and crushed. The total depth of the excavation was 25 cm. The samples were later sieved through 1.5 mm mesh (RJ 1974, FN Bk 1, 63–5).

Chronology

Lower Level was dated from a *Dosinia*/charcoal pair (ANU-2013). A date of 515–130 cal BP was obtained on shell and 505–0 cal BP on charcoal (Table 3.1).

Results

There is a range of both marine and mangrove shellfish present in the upper and lower levels (Appendix 2). The dominant shellfish species by MNI are *Dosinia* and *Marcia* (Table 3.2), by NISP *Dosinia* and *Modiolus* and, by weight, *Dosinia* and *Mactra*. All are marine species, which dominated in both the upper and lower levels, with slightly more emphasis on marine in the lower levels. Mangrove species remain consistently less in both upper and lower levels (Figures 3.1–3.3).

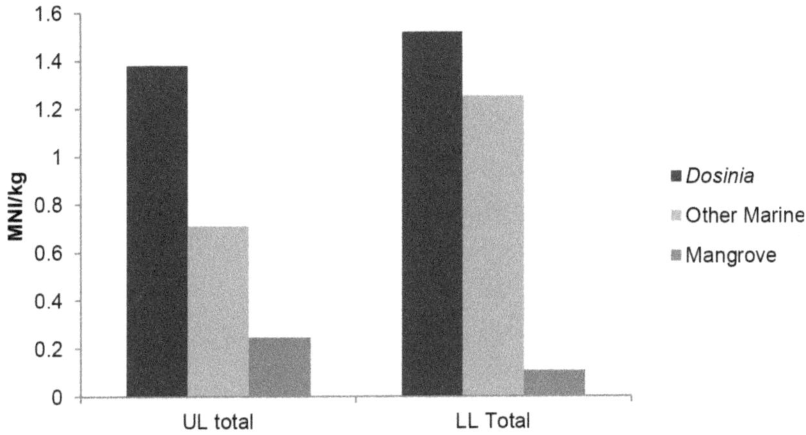

Figure 3.1. *Aningarra*'s Camp shellfish (MNI/kg deposit).

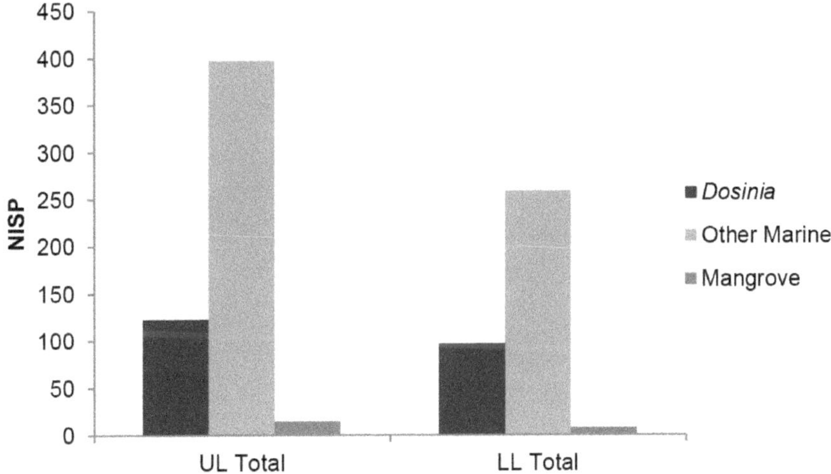

Figure 3.2. *Aningarra*'s Camp shellfish (NISP).

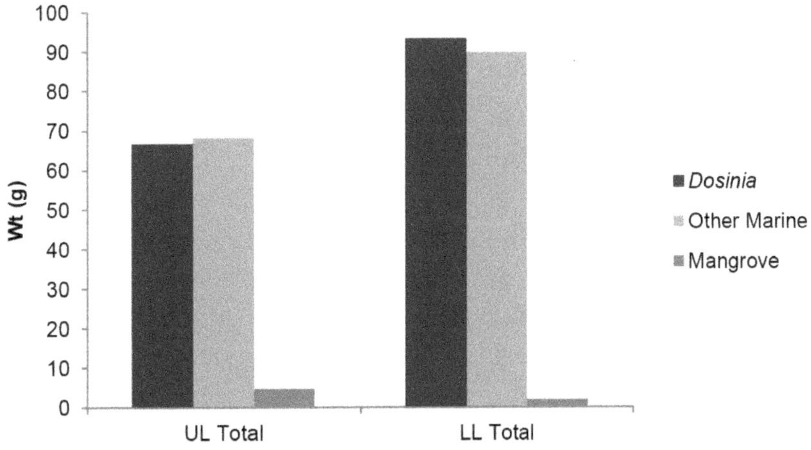

Figure 3.3. *Aningarra*'s Camp shellfish weight (g).

Figure 3.4. *Gulukula* 2015 (Bethune Carmichael).

Gulukula Mounds 1974, 1978

Site description

The *Gulukula* chenier is the base for several large discrete shell mounds up to 5 m in height and 30 m in diameter (Map 2.1, Figure 3.4). Known as the *Gulukula* or Dog Mounds, they are the most famous on *An-barra* land. They lie inland, about 1 km from *Guna-jengga* on the present-day coast, and 2 km west of *An-gartcha Wana* (Map 3.1). "According to the *An-barra*, at some time in the past, the first dog in the country piled up these extensive mounds of shells with his paws, as dogs do with earth when they are digging a hole" (Meehan 1982a, 167).
Frank Gurrmanamana described the mounds as:

> "Too much shell – can't finish him." To demonstrate this, Frank dug a small hole into the corner of one. He did not express any objection to our sampling the midden archaeologically. He thought one midden had grown higher since he was last here – the "Dreaming" is obviously still on-going. Frank expressly denied any human association for the middens – even the question of where the shells had come from (i.e. beach, mangrove etc.) was meaningless as the "Dog Dreaming" had formed them (RJ 1972, FN Bk 9, 18–19).

Excavation

Gulukula was sampled twice, in 1974 and 1978. In 1974, Betty excavated a 50 × 50 cm test pit, 10 m from the top of one of the mounds that she describes as being the largest of the *Gulukula* shell mounds, 5 m high and 50 m wide. The pit was 25 cm in depth. Two solid samples were taken, Bags 1 and 2, as well as a dating sample from the bottom of the pit. There was shell only, no charcoal being obvious (BM 1974, FN Bk 2, 61). The deposit was sieved through 4 mm mesh. In 1978, a solid sample was taken 10 cm below the surface inside a goanna burrow (BM 1978, FN Bk 5, 29). Jones and Chappell took another sample from 25 cm depth in 1999.

Chronology

From *Gulukula* 1974, the shell (*Dosinia*) sample taken from 25 cm gave a date of 875–465 cal BP (ANU-2021). From *Gulukula* 1978, a shell sample (*Dosinia*) taken from 80 cm depth was dated to 666–392 cal BP (Wk-24232) (Table 3.1; Meehan 1983). In 1999, Jones and Chappell took another sample that was dated to 641–312 cal BP (Blyth 299) (Table 3.1).

Results

Gulukula 1974

Both marine and mangrove species (Appendix 2) were in the sample taken from the top of a *Gulukula* Mound in 1974. The dominant species by MNI, NISP and weight were marine, including *Dosinia, Modiolus* and *Mactra* (Table 3.3). In the sample taken from the side of a *Gulukula* Mound, *Dosinia* was the dominant species, and the other species appeared in negligible quantities.

Gulukula 1978

Like the 1974 samples, the dominant species by MNI, NISP and weight were marine, dominated by *Dosinia*. The other species appeared in negligible quantities (Tables 3.4 and 3.5).

Guna-jengga 1974

Guna-jengga, 3 km west of *Lalarr gu-jirrapa*, is associated with an important fish trap, built across a creek flowing into the sea, which was used in the mid-dry season (Map 3.1; Meehan 1982a, 36, 113, 166). Frank Gurrmanamana said it is *rrawa*, a remembered camp site occupied during the "cold weather time" (i.e. not a Dreaming site) (RJ 1973, FN Bk 21, 26).

Rhys described *Guna-jengga* and the fish trap back in 1972:

Table 3.3. *Gulukula* 1974 Bags 1 & 2 Shellfish taxa MNI, NISP & Wt (g).

	Marine										Mangrove						
	Dosinia	*Modiolus*	*Mactra*	*Marcia*	*Tegillarca*	*Nassarius*	*Trisidos*	*Placamen*	*Tellina*		*Terebralia*	*Telescopium*	*Crassostrea*	*Cerithidea*	*Nerita*	*Cassidula*	
Bag 1										**Total**							**Total**
NISP	282	91	36	16	2	4	1	1	1	**434**	9	6	1	10	1	1	**28**
MNI	141	46	18	8	2	4	1	1	1	**222**	9	6	1	10	1	1	**28**
Wt (g)	207	49	65	19.6	6.3	5.4	1.1	0.2	0	**353.6**	21.6	33	12.9	7.3	1	0.6	**76.4**
Bag 2																	
NISP	339	2	6	5	0	0	0	0	0	**352**	5	2	0	0	0	0	**7**
MNI	170	1	5	3	0	0	0	0	0	**179**	5	2	0	0	0	0	**7**
Wt (g)	609.7	1.2	5.5	6.8	0	0	0	0	0	**623.2**	20.4	1.7	0	0	0	0	**22.1**

Then we came to *Gunedjanga* a good camping place about ¾ mile west of *Djunwinia* – country belonging to George Fry (*Darawolnga*) (RJ 1972 FN, Bk 5, 8).

There is a well behind the beach berm and the remains of a hut on the beach… We went to where the fish trap was situated. Tommy remembered it in use when he was a little boy – say 10 or 12. There is a small stream – the upper portion of the one at *Djinaka* (RJ 1972 FN, Bk 5, 8–9).

The stream is tidally inundated even this far up. The stream at this point is in a well defined trench, 5 feet deep and perhaps 10 yds across. The trap was located on a narrow part on a corner… It consisted of a fence of vertical sticks with some kind of wickerwork woven through the sticks about 3 feet high. They formed a V shaped entrance to a funnel – which is a cylindrical basket through which the fish entered the trap – and when the tide went out, they could not find their way out again. Fish caught there were salmon fish, barramundi, "moon fish", prawn, mullet, crab – "big mob". On the other side (i.e. mouth) was a prominent midden with dense shell and charcoal about 2 feet thick in one place. The man who worked the trap lived here. People came to the trap to get fish – from *Kopanga*, *Lalagidjiripa*, *Djunuwinia* and even from

Table 3.4. *Gulukula* 1978 Shellfish taxa NISP, MNI & Wt (g).

		Marine								Mangrove					
		Dosinia	*Marcia*	*Mactra*	*Modiolus*	*Volegalea*	*Tegillarca*	*Placamen*		*Cerithidea*	*Crassostrea*	*Geloina*	*Telescopium*	*Cassidula*	
XU	**Depth (cm)**								**Total**						**Total**
UL	**0–6**	62	14	5	5	5	2	1	**94**	5	3	2	1	0	**11**
LL	**20–25**	57	26	8	5	3	4	1	**104**	1	2	0	0	1	**4**

Table 3.5. *Gulukula* 1974 and 1978 Comparison of shellfish taxa by habitat (MNI).

	Marine											Mangrove					
	Dosinia	*Modiolus*	*Mactra*	*Marcia*	*Nassarius*	*Saccostrea*	*Tegillarca*	*Placamen*	*Tellina*	*Trisidos*		*Cerithidea*	*Terebralia*	*Telescopium*	*Cassidula*	*Nerita*	
											Total MNI						**Total MNI**
1974–1	141	46	18	8	4	1	2	1	1	1	**223**	10	9	6	1	1	**27**
1974–2	170	1	5	3	0	0	0	0	0	0	**179**	0	5	2	0	0	**7**
1978	239	9	16	0	2	2	1	0	0	0	**269**	0	3	7	0	0	**10**

Madangadjire too – and they took fish back in the same day. They brought other food in exchange. The man who worked it was George Fry's father. He is dead now about 3 years ago at Maningrida (an old man). He was a man of this country. Maybe 2 or 3 men and their families used to camp here during the night to work the trap. During the day they would go and "sit down" on the beach etc. Other traps were situated on the same stream, both down and upstream – the latter during the rainy season. All the traps were made by George Fry's father – according to Tommy (RJ 1972 FN, Bk 5, 9 –12).

We got back into the stream bed again and walked and searched westwards until we got to the SE corner of the big coastal sand dune facing the main place of *Gunedjangga*. Here we climbed the near vertical bank about 10 feet high. About 30–50 yds further west, the stream makes another twist which

> brings it against the dune wall again a cliff bank about 8–10 feet high. This is where old man Les Angabarapara used to have a fish trap. The channel is only about 15 feet wide at this point. Tommy Galpadanga told me that they used to camp on the dune near the beach – e.g. 200 yds away, and old man would go and get fish in his trap and bring it back. We walked onto the dune and rested for another smoko (5 mins) under a shady tree. All around us were patches of shells – all acknowledged to be dinner camps. This was part of *Gunedjangga* (RJ 1972 FN, Bk 8, 39).
>
> On the *Gunedjanga* dune there is a well, still cleaned out, about 20 yds N/NW of where the old "Les" fish trap had been. This well was clean and had 1 baler by it, but there was no water in it. All day – we went without water (RJ 1972 FN, Bk 8, 44).

Betty described the use of the fish trap in April 1973:

> … two species of crab and prawns contributed to the crustacea weight, many of these being caught in the fish trap at *Gunadjeng-ga*. Five species of shark and stingray and 16 other species of fish contributed 500 kg gross weight to the diet in April – again, much of this came from the fish trap at *Gunadjenga-ga* (Meehan 1982a, 153).

She went on to say, however, that it was not always reliable:

> Everyone who walks to *Guna-jengga* hopes to have a substantial meal consisting of seafood from the fish trap but may eventually have to gather *Mactra meretriciformis* [now *M. abbreviata*] and *Dosinia juvenilis* because the trap is found to be empty, and several other strategies fail (Meehan 1982a, 112).

Site description

The archaeological site of *Guna-jengga* is a coastal midden consisting of a modern "dinner time" camp overlying an older midden deposit (Figure 3.5). The site is about 200 m from the beach where there is a well behind the beach berm.

Rhys described the site in 1973:

> Given the narrowness of the dunes here – pinched between the sea and the tidal creek behind – viz. only about 50 – 60 yds… this is the only place to camp. During high tides, there would be no foreshore and people would be forced back on the narrow shelf on the front (seaward) slope of the dunes or in little swales amongst them – i.e. exactly where the old midden

Figure 3.5. *Guna-jengga* (Rhys Jones).

now is, plus the present dinner camp. All the beach camp debris would be obliterated by the king tide and so all that is left is the occupation debris on the front apron of the dunes. In this way, the midden corresponds exactly to the front of the *Lalargedjiripa* occupied by the "permanent" *Anbarra* (and in a different place – *Madai*) houses, just above the king tide – to which they all shift during high tides – and from which they fan out to the beach during weak tides. The only difference is that the sand behind the camp at *Lala*... is flat – that at *Gunedjanga* forms a narrow and tussocky, quite steep little ridge – squeezing any occupation tightly to the beach front (RJ 1973, FN Bk 23, 5–6).

> To the west of the tree, from about 10 yds to 50/60 yds west of it and exactly at the same "height" above sea level – as the tree and the "dinner time camp" site – is an outcrop of dense shell midden. This is between 6" and 9" thick and is continuous, in outcrop over 50 yds… In places, the surface of this midden is exposed at the present surface – in the places it is overlain by some recent dune sand. I estimate that its age would be anything from say 25/50 yrs old to 100/150 yrs old (RJ 1973, FN Bk 21, 26–7).
>
> This midden lens is exposed along the dune front for a length of about 60 yds, the eastern edge of it coming to where the present dinner camp is… The present camp debris is laid directly on top of this midden on the west edge of the "dinner camp" and separated from it by about 2–4" of fresh white sand in the east. In the east, the old midden has also been cut away in places by modern wind blown swales plus the dinner camp debris laid on the floor of the "clean" sands thus formed. Thus, both the older midden and the present dinner camp would be recognised archaeologically as belonging to different episodes – but they would be seen as two lenses or units of a single midden (RJ 1973, FN Bk 23, 3–5).

In 1974, Rhys reflected on storm damage at *Guna-jengga*:

> Passing the *Gunedjangga* fishing trap tree, we noticed that heavy winds/waves had eroded the fore-dune slope and half exposed the roots of the shade tree. The interesting thing is that the long exposure of shell midden, noted in our previous survey, is now revealed to go right underneath the roots of the tree and right underneath the dinner time camp on which we had rested and dined, and left our own debris… The midden itself, we had sampled – solid and C^{14} samples. Thus, we have two deposits now stratified directly above each other, separated by sand. The lower prehistoric one – C^{14} samples – and the upper one, for which we and our companions are responsible. The upper one is now itself under about two feet of sand… In the coastal dune exposure, we could see the shell midden (the prehistoric one which we had sampled) extending continuously over about 800–1,000 metres (RJ 1974, FN Bk 2, 14–15).

Sampling

In 1974, Rhys sampled the midden:

> Betty and I cleaned up a section of the shell midden outcropping about 30–40 yds west of the fish trap "dinner time" camp under the tree on the beach.

Figure 3.6. Rhys Jones in the *Guna-jengga* section (Betty Meehan).

> Firstly, we cleaned up a section wall about 10 ft long, revealing a dense shell midden layer about 4–6" thick… We then got a C^{14} sample from it – picking out the charcoal bits with a clean trowel into a plastic bag. Then we took 2 solid soil samples. While excavating, we found a strongly cemented ashy hearth about 1½" thick and 12–15" in diameter. This was on the east side of our section starting about 1" in from the first exposed wall (Figure 3.6).
>
> This midden lens is exposed along the dune front for a length of about 60 yds, the eastern edge of it coming to where the present dinner camp is (RJ 1973, FN Bk 23, 3–5).

Chronology

Rhys speculated on the age of the site when he took the sample: "My guess is that the date will prove to be significantly different from 'modern' but will not have a large antiquity – i.e. of the order of 200–400 yrs BP" (RJ 1973, FN Bk 23, 4). He proved to be correct. A *Dosinia*/charcoal pair (ANU-2020) returned an age of 495–0 and 417–0 cal BP respectively (Table 3.1).

Results

Again, the dominant shellfish is marine, *Dosinia* (Table 3.6, Figure 3.7).

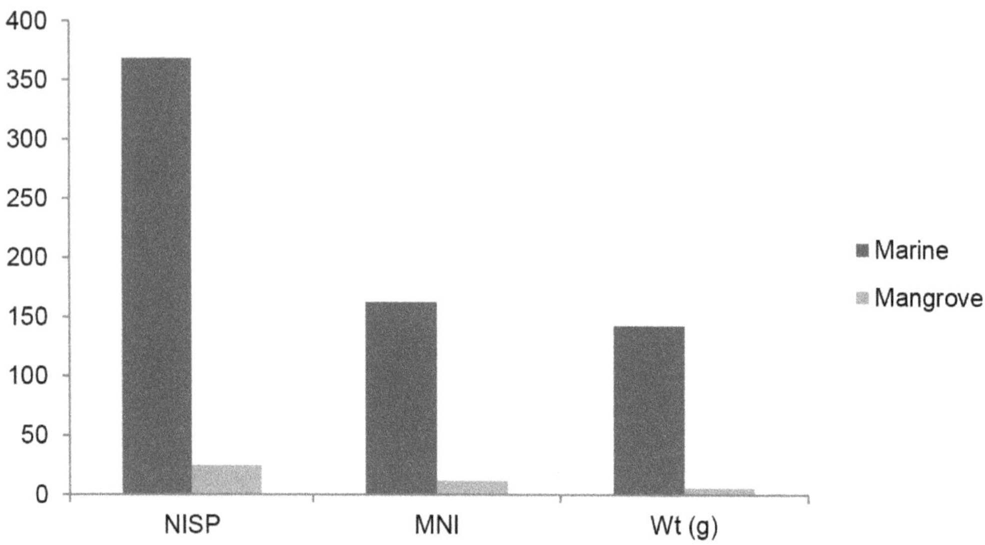

Figure 3.7. *Guna-jengga* Shellfish habitat NISP, MNI & Wt (g).

Table 3.6. *Guna-jengga* Shellfish taxa NISP, MNI & Wt (g).

	Marine								Mangrove				
	Dosinia	*Tellina*	*Modiolus*	*Mactra*	*Marcia*	*Tegillarca*	*Placamen*		*Cerithidea*	*Geloina*	*Telescopium*	*Crassostrea*	
								Total					**Total**
NISP	251	53	50	9	2	2	1	**368**	22	1	1	1	**25**
MNI	127	27	3	2	2	1	1	**163**	9	1	1	1	**12**
Wt (g)	120.1	9.7	4.4	4.2	3.1	0.6	0.2	**142.3**	3.6	1	0.5	0.4	**5.5**

Gupanga wangarr an-dakal a-yurra (where the Dreaming white ochre representing *diyama* lies)

This site is a fossilised shell bed cemented by coarse calcareous sand, containing a mix of shells including *Dosinia* and *Marcia*, exposed intertidally 400 m north of *Gupanga* (Map 3.1; Meehan 1982a, 56).

Rhys described it as follows:

> This "shell rock" is called *Andakul*… and it is the real "dreaming" of *diyama* (*An + Dua*). This *Andakal* is smashed up and the names of places are called

> out, where it is desired that the *diyama* will grow. They go "*dji, dji, dji, dji, dji, dji*" [which is the cry of the whistle duck], then call out the names – *Lalargedjiripa, Moganara* etc. etc. (RJ 1973, FN Bk 16, 72–3).

Betty notes:

> The whistle duck is significant in relation to *diyama* as the patterns on the shells are reminiscent of the markings on the ducks (Meehan 1982a, 52–3).

Chronology

A *Dosinia* sample (ANU-2024) returned an age of 1,695–1,214 cal BP (Table 3.1).

Ji-bena 1979

The earth mound *Ji-bena* is in open woodland adjacent to the freshwater swamp, *Balpilja*, and close to the mangroves lining *An-gartcha Wana*. It is now 8 km from the sea (Maps 2.1, 2.2 and 3.1, Figure 3.8). It is a large circular earth mound approximately 80 m in diameter and 2 m high (Figure 3.9). According to Frank Gurrmanamana, it was occupied in the late wet season (RJ 1979, FN Bk 1, 79).

Excavation

In 1979, Betty and Rhys excavated a metre square test pit in 15 spits that reached 1.65 m in depth (Figures 3.10 and 3.11) (BM 1979, FN Bk 1, 51–89; RJ 1979, FN Bk 1, 57–9, 82–9).

Chronology

Ji-bena was dated to 1,284–790 cal BP (ANU-2817), 10 cm above base. Four other sequential dates were obtained, the youngest being 710–333 cal BP (ANU-2815), 50 cm below the surface (Table 3.1; Brockwell et al. 2005; Meehan 1988a; White et al. 1990).

Results

Shell, bone and stone artefacts were recovered from the *Ji-bena* excavation. Relative quantities are recorded in Table 3.7. Two pieces of glass were also found in Spit 1, maximum depth 8 cm.

Shell

Twenty taxa were identified: the marine taxa *Dosinia, Modiolus, Mactra, Nassarius, Tellina, Volema, Tegillarca, Marcia, Saccostrea, Volegalea, Neverita, Melo amphora, Cymbiola* and *Syrinx*; the mangrove taxa *Cerithidea, Telescopium, Terebralia, Geloina, Cassidula*; and the terrestrial taxon *Xanthomelon*. The relative proportions of taxa are

Figure 3.8. Rhys Jones at the location of *Ji-bena* (Betty Meehan).

Figure 3.9. Rhys Jones at *Ji-bena* earth mound (Betty Meehan).

Figure 3.10. *Ji-bena* excavation (Rhys Jones).

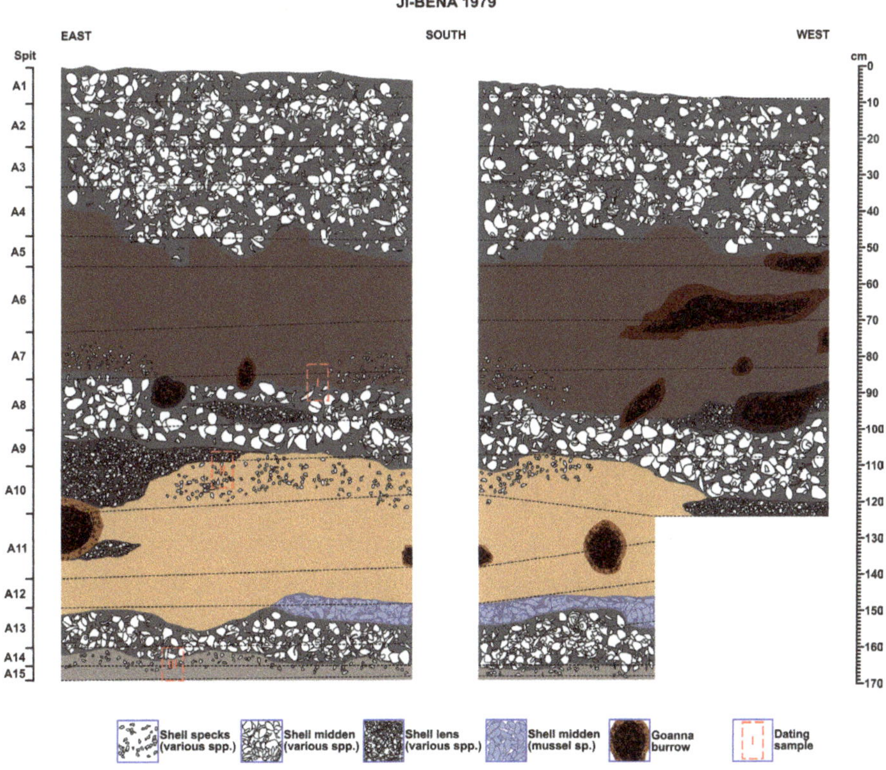

Figure 3.11. *Ji-bena* section (Billy Ó Foghlú).

Table 3.7. *Ji-bena* Quantitative data.

XU	XU Wt (kg)	Spit Size (cm)	Depth (cm)	Shell Wt (g)	Bone Wt (g)	Stone Wt (g)
1	120	8	8	37.7	45.9	376.1
2	210	14	24	23.0	54.1	44.2
3	150	10	33	94.7	22.3	149.7
4	225	15	48	14.3	53.4	311.2
5	120	8	55	1.4	23.0	11.5
6	240	16	73	22.3	5.8	534.7
7	195	13	86	484.6	0.2	0.5
8	210	14	100	997.4	0.0	48.7
9	165	11	111	1065.6	0.8	6.8
10	195	13	123	1010.3	0.0	2.8
11	210	14	136	544.3	0.5	1.2
12	150	10	148	713.3	0.0	0.0
13	165	11	160	1364.7	0.0	0.0
14	90	6	165	972.3	0.0	3.8
15	30	2	169	7.0	0.1	0.0
Total	**2475**	-	-	**7352.9**	**228.7**	**1491.2**

shown in Table 3.8. They are listed with the numerous species first. *Dosinia juvenilis* dominated the assemblage by MNI and weight. Marine shellfish dominated until c. 700 years BP when they disappeared from the assemblage (Figure 3.12).

Other faunal material

A total of 206.1 g of bone was recovered from the *Ji-bena* excavation. Most bone was found in the upper part of the excavation post c. 500 years BP. The distribution is recorded in Table 3.9 and Figure 3.13.

Turtle was the dominant taxon, followed by mammal, fish, reptile and bird (Table 3.10). Identified mammal bone includes the teeth and jaws of the northern brushtail possum (*Trichosurus arnhemensis*), northern brown bandicoot (*Isoodon macrourus*), an unspecified rodent and macropod. Fish bones include the vertebrae,

Table 3.8. *Ji-bena* Total shellfish taxa MNI & Wt (g).

	Taxon	MNI	Wt (g)	% MNI	% Wt
Marine	*Dosinia*	1474	4011.7	80.2	56.7
	Modiolus	122	88.9	6.6	1.3
	Mactra	40	144.6	2.2	2
	Nassarius	39	26.1	2.1	0.4
	Tellina	12	21.4	0.7	0.3
	Volema	8	14.3	0.4	0.2
	Tegillarca	7	31.4	0.4	0.4
	Marcia	7	28.3	0.4	0.4
	Saccostrea	6	33.4	0.3	0.5
	Volegalea	6	24.7	0.3	0.3
	Neverita	6	10.1	0.3	0.1
	Melo amphora	5	52.7	0.3	0.7
	Cymbiola	5	1.7	0.3	0
	Syrinx	1	6.3	0.1	0.1
	barnacle	1	0.8	0.1	0
Mangrove	*Cerithidea*	59	34.9	3.2	0.5
	Telescopium	51	308.7	2.8	4.4
	Terebralia	40	83.9	2.2	1.2
	Geloina	21	419	1.1	5.9
	Cassidula	17	25.8	0.9	0.4
Terrestrial	*Xanthomelon*	8	19.1	0.4	0.3
	No ID	-	1743.6	-	-
	Total	**1935**	**7131.4**	**-**	**-**

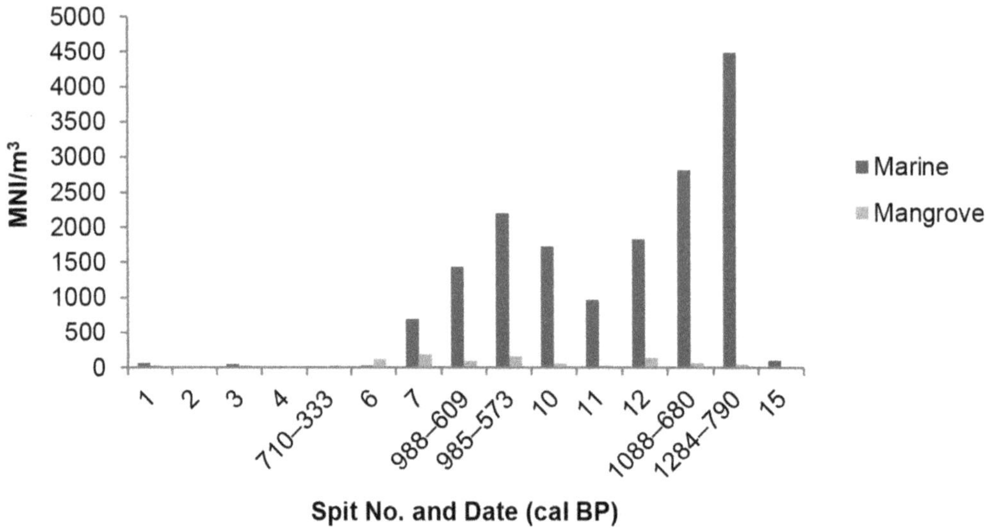

Figure 3.12. *Ji-bena* Chronological distribution of shellfish (MNI/m³).

spines and cranium of two common north Australian fish, the fork-tailed catfish (*Arius* sp.) and barramundi (*Lates calcarifer*). Both species can live in either fresh or saltwater. Neither bird (long bones) nor reptile remains (vertebrae) could be identified to family or species level. Freshwater taxa (turtle) became dominant in the assemblage c. 700 years ago until the recent past (Figure 3.14).

Stone assemblage

Altogether there were 71 stone artefacts weighing 1,496.9 g recovered from the excavation at *Ji-bena*, with an average density of 46.5 artefacts per cubic metre. The artefacts were concentrated in the upper part of the site post 500 years BP (Table 3.11, Figure 3.15). The most common item was flaked quartzite, including one quartzite bipolar core. There were also some ground ochre, haematite and sandstone artefacts (Table 3.12).

Jilangga a-jirra

Jilangga a-jirra is located 3 km from the eastern bank of *An-gartcha Wana*, and about 1 km from the coast (Map 3.1). There is a thin shell midden scatter, located on top of an inland vegetated dune running parallel to the coast. It lies adjacent to a large shell mound, which is a wet season camp belonging to the *Gu-lalay* who are related to the *An-barra*. Stone tools were observed on the surface of the midden, along with mammal and fish bones (Meehan 1982a, 38, 163).

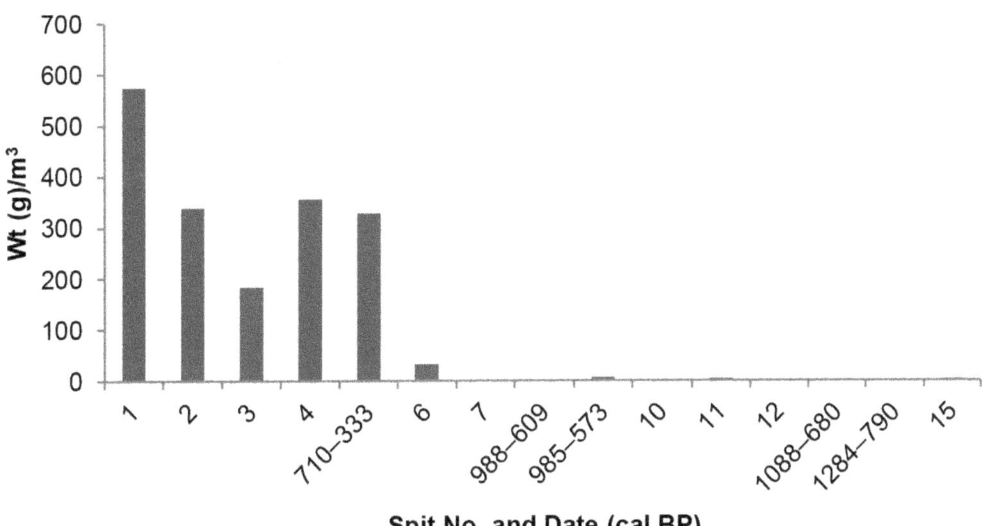

Figure 3.13. *Ji-bena* Chronological distribution of bone (wt g/m³).

Table 3.9. *Ji-bena* Chronological distribution of bone (g/m³ of deposit).

Spit No.	Date (cal BP)	Vol. (m³)	Wt (g)	Wt (g/m³)
1	-	0.08	45.9	573.8
2	-	0.16	54.1	338.1
3	-	0.09	16.6	184.4
4	-	0.15	53.4	356.0
5	710–333	0.07	23.0	328.6
6	-	0.18	5.8	32.2
7	-	0.13	0.2	1.5
8	988–609	0.14	0.0	0.0
9	985–573	0.11	0.8	7.3
10	-	0.12	0.0	0.0
11	-	0.13	0.5	3.8
12	-	0.12	0.0	0.0
13	1088–680	0.12	0.0	0.0
14	1284–790	0.05	0.0	0.0
15	-	0.04	0.1	2.5
	Total	**1.69**	**200.4**	**1828.2**

Table 3.10. *Ji-bena* Chronological distribution of vertebrate fauna (g/m³ of deposit).

Spit No.	Date (cal BP)	Vol. (m^3)	Turtle (g/m^3)	Mammal (g/m^3)	Fish (g/m^3)	Reptile (g/m^3)	Bird (g/m^3)	No ID (g/m^3)
1	-	0.08	155.0	37.5	10.0	0.0	17.5	353.8
2	-	0.16	75.6	58.8	25.0	23.8	8.1	146.9
3	-	0.09	81.1	12.2	8.9	6.7	2.2	73.3
4	-	0.15	131.3	4.0	14.0	18.7	1.3	186.7
5	710–333	0.07	210.0	17.1	1.4	8.6	0.0	91.4
6	-	0.18	26.1	1.1	0.0	0.6	0.0	4.4
7	-	0.13	0.0	0.8	0.0	0.0	0.0	0.8
8	988–609	0.14	0.0	0.0	0.0	0.0	0.0	0.0
9	985–573	0.11	0.0	0.0	0.0	0.0	0.0	7.3
10	-	0.12	0.0	0.0	0.0	0.0	0.0	0.0
11	-	0.13	0.0	0.0	0.0	0.0	0.0	3.8
12	-	0.12	0.0	0.0	0.0	0.0	0.0	0.0
13	1088–680	0.12	0.0	0.0	0.0	0.0	0.0	0.0
14	1284–790	0.05	0.0	0.0	0.0	0.0	0.0	0.0
15	-	0.04	0.0	0.0	0.0	0.0	0.0	2.5
	Total	**1.69**	**679.1**	**131.5**	**59.3**	**58.4**	**29.1**	**870.9**

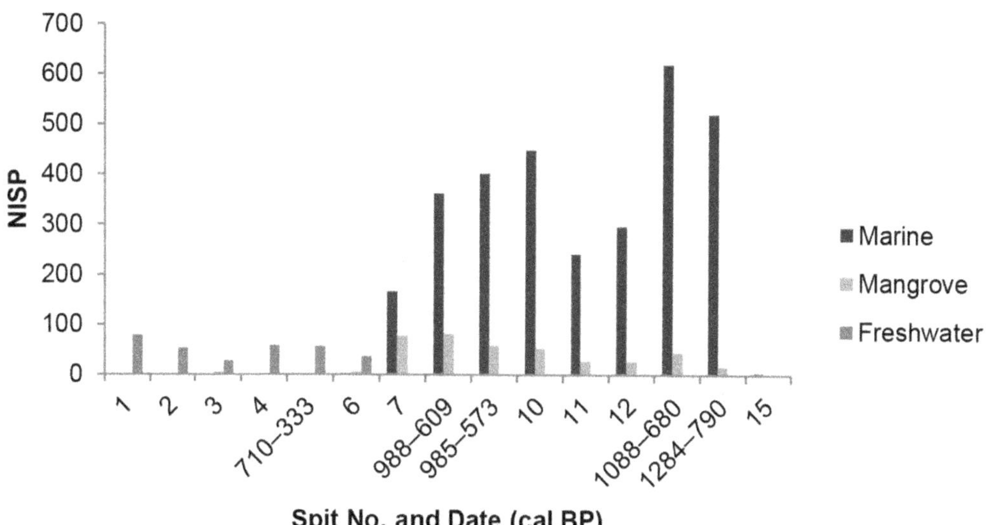

Figure 3.14. *Ji-bena* Chronological distribution of fauna by habitat (NISP).

Table 3.11. *Ji-bena* Chronological distribution of stone artefacts (no. & g/m³ of deposit).

Spit No.	Date (cal BP)	No. of Artefacts	Wt (g)	Vol. (m³)	No./m³
1	-	19	376.1	0.08	237.5
2	-	9	44.2	0.14	64.3
3	-	6	155.4	0.10	60.0
4	-	18	311.2	0.15	120.0
5	710–333	5	11.5	0.08	62.5
6	-	2	534.7	0.16	12.5
7	-	1	0.5	0.13	7.7
8	988–609	7	48.7	0.14	50.0
9	985–573	4	6.8	0.11	36.4
10	-	3	2.8	0.13	23.1
11	-	2	1.2	0.14	14.3
12	-	0	0.0	0.10	0.0
13	1088–680	0	0.0	0.11	0.0
14	1284–790	1	3.8	0.06	16.7
15	-	0	0.0	0.02	0.0
	Total	**77**	**1496.9**	**1.65**	**46.7**

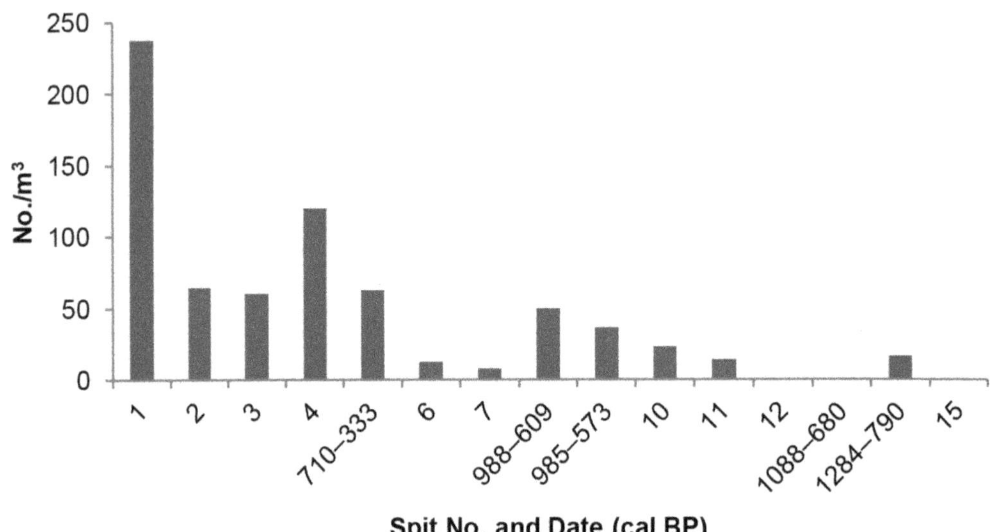

Figure 3.15. *Ji-bena* Chronological distribution of stone artefacts (no./m³).

Table 3.12. *Ji-bena* Chronological distribution of lithic raw materials (nos).

Spit No.	Date (cal BP)	Quartzite	Sandstone	Silcrete	Ochre	Haematite	Shale	Chert
1	-	10	2	3	3	1	0	0
2	-	7	2	0	0	0	0	0
3	-	5	0	0	1	0	0	0
4	-	12	2	1	0	1	2	0
5	710–333	3	1	1	0	0	0	0
6	-	1	0	1	0	0	0	1
7	-	1	0	0	0	0	0	0
8	988–609	6	0	0	0	0	0	0
9	985–573	4	0	0	0	0	0	0
10	-	3	0	0	0	0	0	0
11	-	2	0	0	0	0	0	0
12	-	0	0	0	0	0	0	0
13	1088–680	0	0	0	0	0	0	0
14	1284–790	1	0	0	0	0	0	0
15	-	0	0	0	0	0	0	0
	Total	**55**	**7**	**6**	**4**	**2**	**2**	**1**

Figure 3.16. Bethune Carmichael at *Jinawunya* (Sally Brockwell).

Sampling

A dating sample was taken 15–20 cm from the top of the midden, which had been dug out to make a cooking pit for six wallabies.

Chronology

A *Dosinia*/charcoal pair (ANU-2022) returned dates of 1,235–703 cal BP and 452 to modern cal BP (Table 3.1). The discrepancy in dates could be due to sampling from disturbed deposit.

Jinawunya 1978

Jinawunya is a coastal area on the western side of *An-gartcha Wana*, on the western margin of *An-barra* land near the *Gulukula* shell mounds (Map 3.1, Figure 3.16; Meehan 1982a, 12). It is a camping place, popular for shell-fishing and fishing, and for collecting *Pandanus* nuts, vegetables, fruit and wood from trees on the chenier dune behind the beach (Map 2.1). Rhys and Betty made an archaeological transect here (Meehan 1982a, 107, 110–11, 165; BM 1978 FN, Bk 5, 39–44). No excavation was undertaken at *Jinawunya* but dating samples were taken from the large shell midden on a dune adjacent to the beach.

In 1983, Rhys collected a shell sample (*Dosinia juvenilis*) from 20–30 cm below the surface of the midden. We visited *Jinawunya* in 2015 and collected a shell sample (*Anadara antiquata*) from the surface of the midden, which had been half eroded away by wave action (Figure 3.16). This was the same place where doctoral student Bethune Carmichael (2015) interviewed Betty Ngurrpangurrpa for his film *Places in Peril* regarding her perceptions of climate change. We also collected recently dead shells to be compared with archaeological samples in an isotope analysis study to investigate late Holocene changes in sea surface temperatures.

Chronology

The 1983 shell sample (ANU-11206) was dated to 740–430 cal BP. The 2015 sample (Wk-42262) returned a date of 40–0 cal BP (Table 3.1). The discrepancy in dates is likely due to sampling, as the 1983 sample was taken from below the surface and the 2015 sample from the surface.

Jurnaka 1978

Jurnaka (meaning corner) is located on the coast, west of the mouth of *An-gartcha Wana* in a mangrove area, near where *Jurnaka* Creek flows into it (Map 3.1). A shell mound, measuring 24 × 25 m, was deposited on a small natural rise on the coast. A nearby modern midden contained *diyama* (*Marcia*) and mussels on the surface. The maximum depth of the mound was 0.5 m. There was clean sand underneath, then dense midden to the surface (BM 1978, FN Bk 5, 21–6).

Although oysters (*Saccostrea*) were not important to the *An-barra* diet in terms of quantity, they were highly prized and sought after. Called *an-guljaraba*, they come from mangrove areas around the mouth of *An-gartcha Wana*, one of the most popular areas being *Jurnaka*. Betty explains:

> The *Djunaka* area has been heavily exploited in the recent past. Although in this area shells are small and no longer abundant compared with other areas exploited during the year, it is still used because of its accessibility. The oysters occur in clusters on the trunks of mangrove trees or lie on the mud between them. As men frequently use the *Djunaka* area for line and spear-fishing children tend to play in the adjacent mangroves where they collect *C. amasa* [*S. pyschophilla*], as well as *Nerita lineata* and *Volegalea wardiana* (Meehan 1982a, 99).

> Approximately 82 kg of the 354 kg of fish caught during January [1973] consisted of four species of stingray; 20 other species of fish made up the remaining 272 kg. Much of the fishing was done at the mouth of the *Djunaka* creek with a long net (Meehan 1982a, 153).

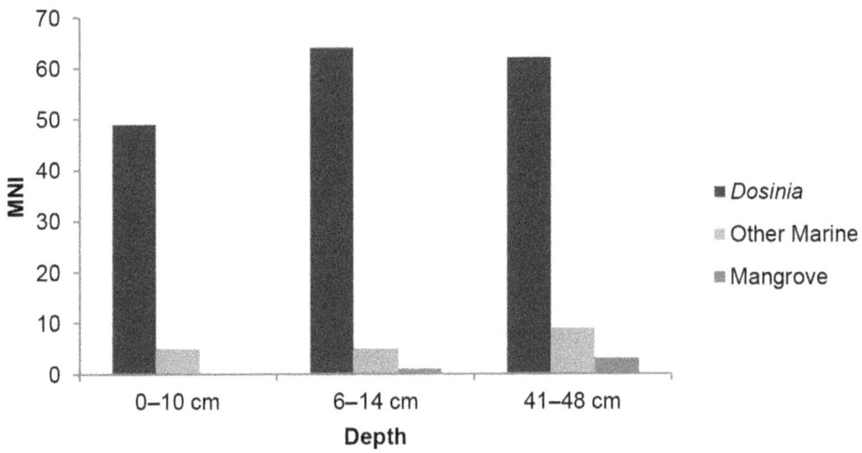

Figure 3.17. *Jurnaka* Distribution of shellfish taxa by habitat (MNI).

Sampling and excavation

The following description of the excavation of the shell mound is taken from Meehan (BM 1978, FN Bk 5, 21–6).

> 0–35 cm – dense shell midden; burnt and broken shell
>
> 35–37 cm – a layer of grey ash, fewer shells
>
> 37–40 cm – two lenses, one 35 cm wide merging into an ash lens 45 cm wide (horizontal features)
>
> 40–46 cm – grey sand with large shells in it; some whole shells on soft dune – "first guys there"?
>
> 50 cm – basal yellow sand
>
> We then took two solid samples – one from the "top" [1–10 cm] and one from the "bottom" [41–48 cm]. We also took charcoal samples from the same units. We also took a sieved shell sample (fine sieved, 2 mm) [6–14 cm]. There was some rootlet penetration in both top and bottom samples (BM 1978 FN, Bk 5, 20–1).

Chronology

A *Dosinia* sample was taken from the base of the shell mound and dated to 373–14 cal BP (Wk-24234) (Table 3.1).

Results

The dominant shellfish was *Dosinia* with other species appearing in low quantities (Table 3.13, Figure 3.17).

Table 3.13. *Jurnaka* 1978 Bags 1, 2 & 3 Distribution of shellfish taxa NISP, MNI, Wt (g).

	Marine								Mangrove		
	Dosinia	*Mactra*	*Placamen*	*Marcia*	*Modiolus*	*Nassarius*	*Tegillarca*		*Cerithidea*	*Terebralia*	
Bag 1, 1–10 cm Bulk Sample								**Total**			**Total**
NISP	97	0	1	1	0	2	1	**102**	0	0	**0**
MNI	49	0	1	1	0	2	1	**54**	0	0	**0**
Wt (g)	119.8	0	1.1	3.9	0	0.6	0.6	**126**	0	0	**0**
Bag 2, 6–14 cm Sieved Sample											
NISP	128	4	3	0	0	0	0	**135**	0	1	**1**
MNI	64	3	2	0	0	0	0	**69**	0	1	**1**
Wt (g)	202.41	13.1	2.7	0	0	0	0	**218.21**	0	1.3	**1.3**
Bag 3, 41–48 cm Bulk Sample											
NISP	123	6	1	3	3	0	1	**137**	3	0	**3**
MNI	62	3	1	2	2	0	1	**71**	3	0	**3**
Wt (g)	113.1	15.5	0.3	9.3	0.9	0	10.7	**149.8**	1.6	0	**1.6**

Lorrkon a-jirrapa East and West 1974

The *Lorrkon a-jirrapa* coastal shell middens are located on a chenier ridge 3 km from the western bank of *An-gartcha Wana* and 2 km from the coast (Maps 2.1 and 3.1). The northern edge is bordered by a salt clay pan, and the southern side is black soil plain. A jungle vine thicket is situated at its base. The midden area is extensive, over 400 m long and 3 m high.

Betty and Rhys describe the site:

> The *Larrakun-adjirripa* area is very midden rich. We found four quartzite flakes on the surface without really looking (BM 1978, FN Bk 5, 2).
>
> … I came to the East/West dune. Here the berm of the dune is encased in an almost continuous capping of dense shell midden. *Larkun Adjiripa* [place of the coffin] is somewhere along this dune to the west… I turn west along the base of the dune, screened by the mangroves at their edge – and am re-impressed by the magnitude of the middens – vast monuments to a dead landscape (RJ 1974, FN Bk 2, 44–6).

Table 3.14. *Lorrkon a-jirrapa* East & West 1974 Shellfish taxa NISP, MNI & Wt (g).

		Lorrkon a-jirrapa East 1974			*Lorrkon a-jirrapa* West 1974		
		NISP	**MNI**	**Wt (g)**	**NISP**	**MNI**	**Wt (g)**
Marine	*Modiolus*	1168	259	57.9	6	1	0.2
	Dosinia	390	195	587.2	272	136	201.3
	Tellina	83	47	38	0	0	0
	Saccostrea	40	13	21.7	0	0	0
	Mactra	30	19	16.3	72	19	43.9
	Nassarius	4	4	0.8	0	0	0
	Neverita	1	1	5.5	0	0	0
	Placamen	1	1	0.2	5	2	2.6
	Volegalea	1	1	0.1	0	0	0
	Marcia	0	0	0	7	5	7.8
	Tegillarca	0	0	0	4	2	1.8
	Total	**1718**	**540**	**727.7**	**366**	**165**	**257.6**
Mangrove	*Telescopium*	29	8	21	16	6	2.7
	Cerithidea	12	10	3.1	0	0	0
	Terebralia	2	2	3.4	8	4	2.5
	Cassidula	2	2	2.6	0	0	0
	Nerita	1	1	2.1	1	1	0.3
	Total	**46**	**23**	**32.2**	**25**	**11**	**5.5**

The huge shell midden capping the E/W dune, I am calling *Larkun Adjiripa* West. It is continuous for 500 metres in most places 4.5 feet… Its width… is at least 25 metres. In one place its width at the flat top of the midden is 35 metres, at base 50 metres. A dense jungle on the plain/south side – jungle clothes ½ the top and south slope of the midden (RJ 1974, FN Bk 2, 49–51).

Then I walked about 200–300 metres east of the eastern edge the midden and came across another big one – circular – with a flat top 35 metres in diameter, ht is 2½–3 ft of shell midden above the dune… The second midden I called *Larkun Adjiripa* East. Again a jungle patch on the south

> edge of it. Really, there are middens extending intermittently all along the crest of this dune from somewhere south… (RJ 1974, FN Bk 2, 52).

Sampling

At *Lorrkon A-Jirrapa* West, Betty and Rhys excavated a 50 cm square test pit to a depth of 30 cm in the middle of the midden. A bulk sample was taken from 20–25 cm.

At *Lorrkon a-jirrapa* East, a midden sample was taken 10–20 cm below the surface (RJ 1974, FN Bk 2, 52).

Chronology

A *Dosinia*/charcoal pair (ANU-2012) was taken from the bulk sample at *Lorrkon a-jirrapa* West 1974 and returned dates of 1,179–750 and 1,345–740 cal BP respectively (Table 3.1).

Results

In both the East and West shell midden samples, *Dosinia* was the dominant shellfish. However, *Lorrkon a-jirrapa* East also had a high proportion of *Modiolus*. Both samples showed mangrove exploitation (Table 3.14).

Lorrkon a-jirrapa West 1978

Lorrkon a-jirrapa West was surveyed and excavated in 1978 (RJ 1978, FN Bk 1, 54; BM 1978, FN Bk 5, 36–9).

Excavation and sampling

> Went and did the excavation of the large midden of *Larkun Adjiripa* West and worked hard – depth 90 cm – pit 60 cm × 60 cm – dense midden on clean yellow beach sand. A quartzite flake in the bottom spit. Lots of little fish bones… some few bits of large mammal, some rat-like bones, one bird bone – some worked shells (RJ 1978, FN Bk 1, 38; BM 1978, FN Bk 5, 2).

The following description of the excavation comes from Betty's field notes (BM 1978, FN Bk 5, 2–3).

> <u>LA/W 1, Spit 1 (1–10 cm depth)</u>
>
> This spit contained shells, small fish bones and a mammal bone; no charcoal. We took a solid sample, collected fish bones etc. and anything that looked interesting, i.e., stones that looked as if they might have use wear on them.

LA/W 1, Spit 2 (10–30 cm)

There is charcoal in this spit which we have collected – also small fish bones and shells. Have found several small concentrations of fish bones, which we have kept together rolled in toilet paper. One lot were small vertebrae. From this spit we have the following bags: charcoal, special finds (fish bones etc.), a shell sample and a solid sample. The NW and NE corners = 25 cm in depth; the SW and SE corners were 30 cm in depth. We dug down through loose shells and grey ashy deposit.

LA/W 1, Spit 3 (30–50 cm)

This spit was rich in thick ash. It also contained quite a few mammal bones, apart from shells, fish bones and lots of charcoal. The bottom of the spit was 50 cm deep.

LA/W 1, Spit 4 (50–80 cm)

This was a dense spit with lots of fine, broken shells and lots of ash. We found one quartzite flake in this spit too. The base of the spit was 80 cm from top. The first appearance of yellow sand appeared there too. It is about 95 cm to the yellow sand. The base pit was one metre.

LA/W 1, Spit 5 (80–90 cm)

In the NE corner, we dug out the wall to obtain one bucket of a deposit. There was some sandy midden below the sand lens and above the yellow sand base. The depth was 80–90 cm. We got one bucket which was double sieved but not sorted. There was lots of charcoal in it (which we collected) in large lumps – first occupation on the beach?

Chronology

A shell sample (*Dosinia juvenilis*) (Wk-24233) was taken from Spit 5 (80–90 cm) at the base of the excavation and dated to 1,166–821 cal BP. Jones and Chappell took two additional shell samples from the midden cap in 1999. They were dated to 1,433–1,046 (Blyth 499) and 1,228–772 cal BP (Blyth 599) (Table 3.1).

Results

Only the shellfish from *Lorrkon a-jirrapa* were analysed, not the fish and mammal bone, stone artefacts or worked shell mentioned by Rhys in his field notes. They are available at the MAGNT in Darwin.

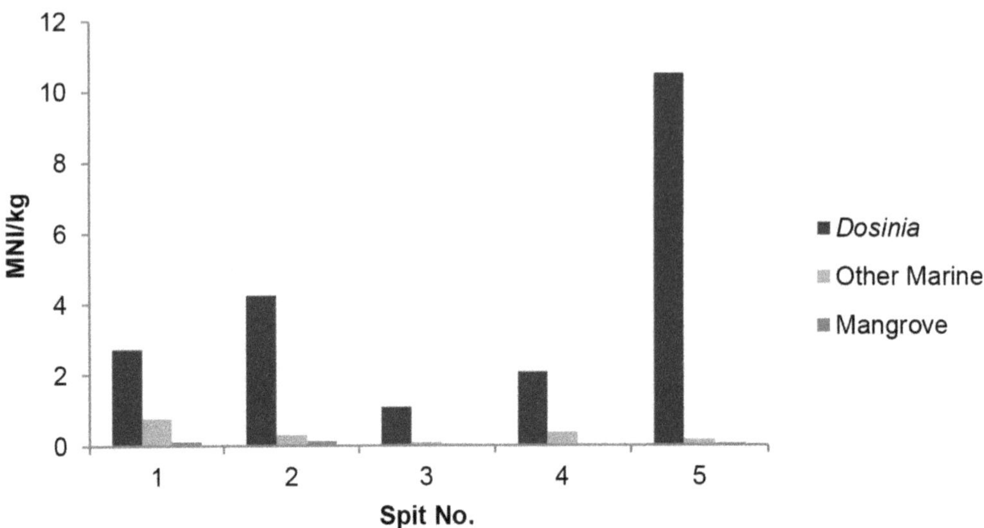

Figure 3.18. *Lorrkon a-jirrapa* West 1978 Shellfish by habitat (MNI/kg deposit).

There are a wide variety of marine and estuarine shellfish represented in the *Lorrkon a-jirrapa* West 1978 excavation. However, *Dosinia* and other marine species dominate all levels by MNI, NISP and weight (Table 3.15, Figure 3.18).

Mu-garnbal 1973

The site of *Mu-garnbal* lies on the east side of *An-gartcha Wana*, about 5 km from the coast at the juncture of the mangroves and the black soil plain (Map 3.1).

Mu-garnbal is owned by the *Martay*. Betty describes the site and its environment:

> The *Matai* [*Martay*] own no coastal sites. Their country is situated on the eastern bank of *An-gartcha Wana* and up to about 12 km from the coast in the mangrove, black soil plain and eucalypt woodland area. At least five different riverside and inland sites were lived in, four of which I was able to visit. *Maganbal* is within a few metres, and on the eastern side, of an extensive area of mangroves growing on the eastern bank of the Blyth River, its main advantage being that during the full blast of the *barra* (northwest monsoon) it is in the lee of this formidable barrier. The camp itself was erected on a dense midden 35 m^2 in area and up to 1 m thick. The posts of the houses had been dug into the shells; the debris of 1973 [cyclone] formed only the top layer of a deposit extending back into prehistory. Black soil plains, inundated during the wet season, surround the site on all but the western side, where mud flats and mangroves clothe the riverbank (Meehan 1982a, 30).

Table 3.15. *Lorrkon a-jirrapa* West 1978 Distribution of shellfish taxa NISP, MNI & Wt (g).

	Marine								Mangrove			
	Dosinia	*Mactra*	*Modiolus*	*Nassarius*	*Saccostrea*	*Tegillarca*	*Volegalea*		*Telescopium*	*Terebralia*	*Nerita*	
Spit 1 Depth 10 cm								**Total**				**Total**
NISP	491	103	30	2	2	0	1	**629**	8	1	0	**9**
MNI	245	52	15	2	2	0	1	**317**	7	1	0	**8**
Wt (g)	446.5	35.8	5.2	3.7	5.2	0	55.4	**551.8**	21.9	2.5	0	**24.4**
Spit 2 Depth 30 cm												
NISP	1531	74	27	0	3	1	1	**1637**	18	3	1	**22**
MNI	765	37	14	0	3	1	1	**821**	17	3	1	**21**
Wt (g)	1922.3	73.8	9.6	0	9.9	4.8	14.6	**2035**	109.7	4.4	4.5	**118.6**
Spit 3 Depth 50 cm												
NISP	393	19	7	1	0	2	0	**422**	4	1	0	**5**
MNI	197	11	4	1	0	1	0	**214**	4	1	0	**5**
Wt (g)	722	19.5	2.5	1.6	0	12.8	0	**758.4**	7.8	1.7	0	**9.5**
Spit 4 Depth 80 cm												
NISP	1129	89	80	9	0	3	0	**1310**	13	0	2	**15**
MNI	564	45	41	9	0	2	0	**661**	11	0	2	**13**
Wt (g)	1313.4	106.6	9.3	5.7	0	11.9	0	**1446.9**	38.6	0	8.5	**47.1**
Spit 5 Depth 90 cm												
NISP	1891	16	11	0	0	1	0	**1919**	1	4	0	**5**
MNI	945	8	6	0	0	1	0	**960**	1	4	0	**5**
Wt (g)	849	34.3	3.8	0	0	15.4	0	**902.5**	1.3	6	0	**7.3**

Table 3.16. *Mu-garnbal* Bags 1 & 2 Shellfish taxa NISP, MNI & Wt (g) XU.

	Marine				Mangrove				
	Tegillarca	*Dosinia*	*Mactra*		*Terebralia*	*Telescopium*	*Nerita*	*Cassidula*	
				Total					**Total**
NISP	304	1	1	**306**	21	10	2	1	**34**
MNI	152	1	1	**154**	21	10	2	1	**34**
Wt (g)	1083.7	1.1	21.8	**1106.6**	67.3	176	4.6	1.1	**249**

> During the 1972–73 wet season the *Matai* camped for a time at *Maganbal* on a small shell midden mound about 25 m by 10 m in area and 0.6 m thick situated on the boundary between a black soil plain and a bank of mangroves backing onto the Blyth River (Meehan 1982a, 167).

The site is named after a canoe as described in Rhys' field notes:

> In the mid-morning *Moganbal* [the canoe] came in with the high tide and moored. In it were David B, Mary M and Laurie M and Jimmy. They had come to pick up the rest of their gear. They are now camped on top of a *gun-apila* [mound] at or near *Maganbal*, close to the forest. They have some houses made from *gangula* [Arafura palm] fronds. They have been making *datcho* [cake] from the cycad trees in the woods. Also, they had been hunting *jin-gombula* [mouse] and *jarrka* [goanna] in the hollows and swamps of the *kapal* [black soil plains]. The camp at *Maganbal* consists of… 5 men, 4 women and 5 kids = 14 (RJ 1973, FN Bk 14, 73).

Sampling

Betty and Rhys recorded *Mu-garnbal* and took a sample from its low dense midden on 27–29 June 1973 (Meehan 1975, Appendix 4, p. A33).

Chronology

A *Tegillarca granosa* sample (Wk-17746) was dated to 3,724–3,345 cal BP (Table 3.1).

Results

The sample from *Mu-garnbal* is dominated by *Tegillarca*, a marine species, with some mangrove species (Table 3.16).

Muyu a-jirrapa Coastal Shell Midden 1974, 1978

Site description

Muyu a-jirrapa lies on the west bank of *An-gartcha Wana*, 1 km from its mouth and c. 1 km north of *Gupanga*. There is a linear midden 500 m long (Figure 3.19), with a shell mound behind (Figure 3.20). The midden was stratified on top of a sand dune and covered by jungle thicket in some parts. The edge of the midden was being eroded by the river. It was recorded by Betty and Rhys in 1974 and excavated in 1978 (Figures 3.21 and 3.22). It was still used occasionally as a camping and cooking site in 1973–74.

The site was described by both Betty and Rhys:

> About 4.30 pm we went to [do] some work on the eroding dune (coastal midden) at *Miadjirripa*. It is about 12" thick and comes almost to the present-day surface. Right on top of this midden there was a "recent" hearth with crab, fish and *angalidjauwurigia* [*Tegillarca*] remains visible in it. We also noticed a *gungapila* [mound] inland and to the south of this site; it was shell covered and a small, jungle-type vegetation and fruit trees were growing upon it (BM 1974, FN Bk 1, 90) (Figure 3.19).

> Very high seas actually reach the base of the cutting, but usually, a beach of some 4 m separates it from most high tides (RJ 1974, FN Bk 1, 84).

> In depth, the midden ranged from 23 cm to 30 cm… about 1 metre above the normal high water mark. My exposed section was 7 metres long. However, the total length of the dense midden is 75 metres along the wave cut beach berm edge – and it extends in from the berm edge distances variously: 8 metres, 12 metres, 15 metres, 4 metres. The midden is called *Miadjirripa* Coast 1974 (RJ 1974, FN Bk 1, 83–4) (Figure 3.20).

> The top of the midden formed the top of the "dune", and here, on the berm edge, immediately above where we took the sample was a modern… hearth 1 × 1½ metres – with remains of crab and fish… There was also another cooking hearth, about 6 m in from the berm and 2 m south of the 1st hearth… Several small jungle patches – on the midden (RJ 1974, FN Bk 1, 85).

By 1979, the midden was mostly destroyed: "The sea had eroded it [with] two large scallops into the beach/midden edge – last *Barra* [wet season] – no doubt held up by uprooted trees – will go next *Barra*" (RJ 1979, FN Bk 1, 26).

Figure 3.19. Rhys Jones at the *Muyu a-jirrapa* Coastal Shell Midden (Betty Meehan).

Figure 3.20. *An-barra* children sorting finds at *Muyu a-jirrapa* Shell Mound (Betty Meehan).

Figure 3.21. *Muyu a-jirrapa* Coastal Shell Midden 1978 survey (Betty Meehan).

Figure 3.22. *An-barra* children at *Muyu a-jirrapa* Coastal Shell Midden 1978 excavation (Betty Meehan).

Sampling 1974

The shell midden was sampled for dating in 1974:

> In the late afternoon, Betty and I went to get shell samples and C^{14} from a large shell midden, whose edge can be seen eroding on the beach berm about 400 yds north of the present Kopanga camp – I cleaned up the section. The midden was dense – lots of burnt shell – mostly *anderabula* [*Dosinia*] with a few *diama* [*Marcia*] plus *djinagorongora* [*Mactra*], the odd mussel and small *andjelobaikuda* [*Syrinx*]. The deposit itself was very black and blackened fringes showed that there was a lot of finely comminuted charcoal in it. However actual specks of charcoal are very rare (RJ 1974, FN Bk 1, 83).

Rhys took three solid samples and one small extra carbon sample from a depth of 20–25 cm (RJ 1974, FN Bk 1, 84).

Survey and excavation 1978

The site was surveyed and excavated in 1978 (BM 1978, FN Bk 5, 45–6) (Figure 3.22). The excavation is described by Betty in her field notes (BM 1978, FN Bk 5, 55–73):

> A one metre square was laid out and excavated in six spits. The deposit was sieved through 2 mm mesh (BM 1978 FN, Bk 5, 55).
>
> <u>Spit 1 (0–6 cm)</u>
>
> This spit consists of black sand and not very many shells. Some mussels (from surface hearth above?). Lots of rootlet penetration (BM 1978, FN Bk 5, 56–7).
>
> <u>Spit 2 (6–16.5 cm)</u>
>
> Shells are becoming more numerous. There are some fish bones in this spit. Dense midden deposit in eastern half of square (BM 1978, FN Bk 5, 57–8).
>
> <u>Spit 3 (16.5–25 cm)</u>
>
> The deposit is crammed with shells, whole valves, and burnt and broken pieces. There [is] not much charcoal but some small fish bones (BM 1978, FN Bk 5, 58–61).
>
> <u>Spit 4 (25–35 cm)</u>
>
> Shells are whole and broken into small pieces… The matrix is becoming less compacted and solid, and more loose and sandy… At the end of spit 4, we are approaching clean sand (BM 1978, FN Bk 5, 63–5).

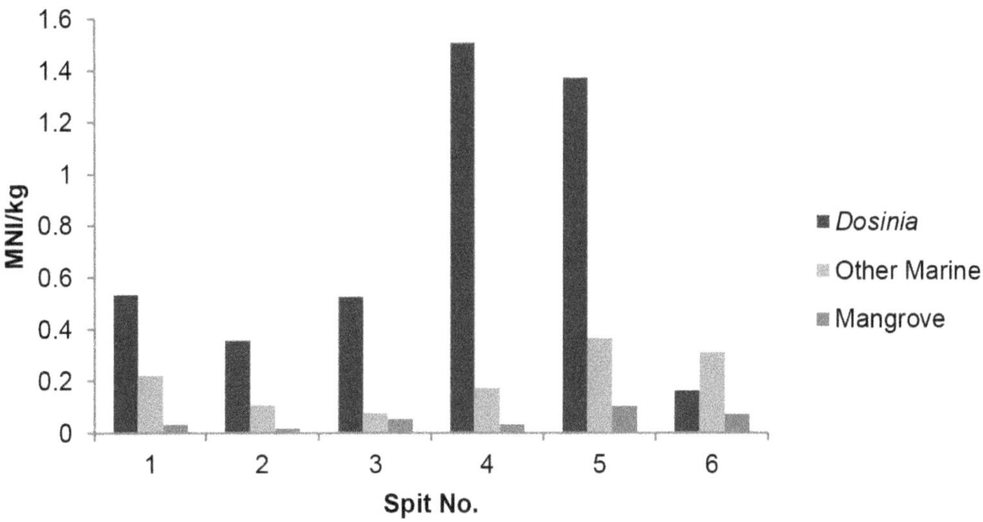

Figure 3.23. *Muyu a-jirrapa* Coastal Shell Midden 1978 Shellfish by habitat (MNI/kg).

> <u>Spit 5 (35–44 cm)</u>
>
> The matrix is now much lighter i.e., moving into yellow sand. Many fewer shells (BM 1978, FN Bk 5, 65–6).
>
> <u>Spit 6</u>
>
> Shells are much scarcer in this spit. There is a lot of rootlet penetration… (BM 1978, FN Bk 5, 67–8).

Chronology

A date of 1,392–987 cal BP (ANU-2014) was obtained from the 1974 *Dosinia* sample (Table 3.1).

Results

Dosinia was the dominant shellfish, both by MNI and weight, with some mangrove species (Tables 3.17 and 3.18, Figure 3.23).

Table 3.17. *Muyu a-jirrapa* Coastal Shell Midden 1978 Distribution of shellfish taxa (MNI).

	Marine										Mangrove							
	Dosinia	*Marcia*	*Nassarius*	*Mactra*	*Modiolus*	*Tegillarca*	*Tellina*	*Placamen*	*Volegalea*		*Cerithidea*	*Telescopium*	*Geloina*	*Cassidula*	*Crassostrea*	*Nerita*	*Terebralia*	
Spit										**Total MNI**								**Total MNI**
1	48	0	1	6	6	2	5	0	0	**68**	0	1	1	1	0	0	0	**3**
2	56	10	0	1	4	2	0	0	0	**73**	0	1	1	0	1	0	0	**3**
3	67	1	0	6	1	0	2	0	0	**77**	0	2	1	0	1	2	1	**7**
4	226	14	4	2	1	1	0	3	1	**252**	4	1	0	0	0	0	0	**5**
5	185	11	9	11	3	7	3	4	1	**234**	13	1	0	0	0	0	0	**14**
6	27	19	18	3	5	1	3	1	1	**78**	11	0	0	1	0	0	0	**12**
Total MNI	**609**	**55**	**32**	**29**	**20**	**13**	**13**	**8**	**3**		**28**	**6**	**3**	**2**	**2**	**2**	**1**	

Table 3.18. *Muyu a-jirrapa* Coastal Shell Midden 1978 Distribution of shellfish taxa Wt (g).

	Marine									
	Dosinia	*Marcia*	*Mactra*	*Tegillarca*	*Tellina*	*Modiolus*	*Placamen*	*Nassarius*	*Volegalea*	
Spit										**Total Wt (g)**
1	102.2	0.0	25.1	1.3	14.4	1.7	0.0	0.3	0.0	**145.0**
2	114.7	45.5	4.1	7.3	0.0	4.9	0.0	0.0	0.0	**176.5**
3	128.7	6.3	12.8	0.0	3.2	0.2	0.0	0.0	0.0	**151.2**
4	583.3	49.9	5.4	1.9	0.0	1.2	3.5	2.7	2.7	**650.6**
5	487.5	21.0	12.5	16.6	1.7	3.4	5.9	2.3	2.0	**552.9**
6	18.2	9.6	1.4	1.1	3.7	7.4	2.4	6.1	0.5	**50.4**
Total Wt (g)	**1434.6**	**132.3**	**61.3**	**28.2**	**23**	**18.8**	**11.8**	**11.4**	**5.2**	
	Mangrove									
	Telescopium	*Crassostrea*	*Cerithidea*	*Geloina*	*Cassidula*	*Nerita*	*Terebralia*			
1	0.1	0.0	0.0	5.1	0.3	0.0	0.0			**5.5**
2	0.7	14.7	0.0	0.6	0.0	0.0	0.0			**16.0**
3	10.0	0.7	0.0	1.6	0.0	2.3	0.6			**15.2**
4	2.5	0.0	1.8	0.0	0.0	0.0	0.0			**4.3**
5	3.3	0.0	3.8	0.0	0.0	0.0	0.0			**7.1**
6	0.0	0.0	2.4	0.0	2.3	0.0	0.0			**4.7**
Total Wt (g)	**16.6**	**15.4**	**8.0**	**7.3**	**2.6**	**2.3**	**0.6**			

Muyu-a-jirrapa Shell Mound 1974, 1978

Site description

Muyu a-jirrapa Shell Mound is small with a dense deposit of shell, located on the western bank of *An-gartcha Wana* about 2 km from its mouth. Rhys described the site:

> In the late afternoon we went to *Meadjiripa* and looked at the shell mound on the dune (RJ 1974, FN Bk 1, 88–9).
>
> [It has] a diameter of 25 m; total height – 70 cm… its east edge about 30 m from the beach – covered with light jungle – a midden scatter all the way to the beach in front. This mound was 75 m north of the north edge of the coastal berm midden exposure – "*Miadjiripa* 1 – beach" – samples taken a few days ago; 40 m, S/SW of the tree at the berm edge, at which FG/Nancy, Betty M etc. had cooked barramundi in 1973 (RJ 1974, FN Bk 1, 90).

Sampling 1974

> I dug a 30 cm square hole in the top of the mound – really shelly… and black matrix. Dug down to 60 cm and took two solid samples from these – called "*Miadjirripa* 2 Mound 1974". Here the deposit was shelly and light grey – perhaps leached of humic content… (RJ 1974, FN Bk 1, 90) (Figure 3.24).
>
> Note, there is another shell midden lateral deposit exposed in the beach berm close to the present camp – it is probably connected to the *Anangara* midden – extends along berm – a distance of some 70 metres – not as thick as the "*Miadjiripa* Beach berm 1" midden. On the KP dune, there are lots of midden scatters – mostly shells nowadays found – *diama* [*Marcia*], *djinagoronggora* [*Mactra*], a few *ngaliwinya* [*Placuna*], and sporadic *angaldjerka* [*Saccostrea*] oysters (RJ 1974, FN Bk 1, 91).

Excavation 1978

Muyu a-jirrapa Shell Mound was excavated by Betty in 1978 in a metre square (BM 1978, FN Bk 5, 81–2, 88–99). The excavation reached a depth of 80 cm in eight spits onto clean sand.

Chronology

Rhys speculated on the date: "It is quite possible that this mound is older than the other *Kopanga* middens tested" (RJ 1974, FN Bk 1, 90). And, indeed, he was correct. A *Dosinia juvenilis* sample taken from the lowest level of the 1978 excavation yielded a date of 1,356–867 cal BP (ANU-2816) (Table 3.1).

Figure 3.24. *Muyu a-jirrapa* Shell Mound 1974 sampling (Rhys Jones).

Results

Unfortunately, this assemblage was lost in the Canberra bushfires of 2003 when ANU's Weston store was burnt to the ground and was never analysed. However, we do have Betty's notes from the excavation that give some idea of the contents of the shell mound. Shells included:

- *Ana-mula an-ika* [*Terebralia*]
- *An-bambula* [*Geloina*]
- *An-demburela* [*Tellina*]
- *An-dirrbula* [*Dosinia*]
- *An-guljuraba* [*Saccostrea*]
- *An-jalabaykarda* [*Melongenidae*]
- *Diyama* [*Marcia*]
- *Ngandipurdurda* [*Tegillarca*]
- *Nornda* [*Telescopium*]
- *Ana-jirralanggula* [*Cymbiola*]

Some shells were very small, especially *an-dirrbula*. Rhys' observation from his 1974 sample is that the mound contained "mostly small *Anderabula*" (RJ 1974, FN Bk 1, 90).

Ngarli ji-bama 1974

Site description

Ngarli ji-bama is a home base on an inland dune associated with fossil shell beds. It is located 4 km east of *An-gartcha Wana*, and about 1 km from the coast, and is occupied in the dry season (Figure 2.1; Maps 2.2 and 3.1). It has a good supply of water from wells surrounding the site. Although it lies close to the sea, the main shell beds (*Modiolus micropterus* [now *modulaides*]) lie 3 km away (Meehan 1982a, 31, 66–7). It is a large open site with a series of shallow midden deposits strung around the circumference. They contain burnt clay, hearth material and shells.

> *Ngalidjibama*, a *Djowanga* moiety site, is situated about 6.5 km east of the Blyth River and 1 km from the coast. The camp site lies where the inland sand dune complex with its alternating parallel dunes and swales meets the eucalypt woodland. This woodland has a boundary zone consisting of several edible fruit trees – for example *Sterculia quadrifolia*, *Pandanus* and *Terminalia carpentariae* – and its understory is dominated by the important food plant *Cycas media*. The camp occupies a largely treeless area 300 m by 100 m on the crest of a dune but is surrounded by dense jungle thickets which include trees such as the banyan (*Ficus virens*) in the shade of which grow a tangle of yams (*Dioscorea*) and other vines. A low rocky ridge, encompassing *Lawuk-adjirripa* (stone-spear-point-place), the only stone quarry in *Gidjingali* country, skirts its western edge and continues south into the forest... Ample evidence for past human occupation is visible on the camp site surface... A string of freshwater holes, excavated up to 1.5 m into shelly deposits, surround the site (Meehan 1982a, 26–7).

> There were lots of chunks of stone visible around *Ngalidjibama*. One had very distinct traces of red ochre still on it (BM 1974, FN Bk 3, 82).

Sampling

"Rhys went off to have a look at some old sites (and, hopefully to take some shell samples)" (BM 1974, FN Bk 3, 2). In 1974, a solid sample was taken from a midden by a banyan tree, one of a series of shallow midden deposits from the large open site. It was sieved through 1.5 mm mesh.

Chronology

A *Mactra abbreviata* sample was dated to 286–0 cal BP (Wk-17747) (Table 3.1).

Table 3.19. *Ngarli ji-bama* Shellfish taxa NISP, MNI & Wt (g).

	Marine									Mangrove				
	Mactra	*Dosinia*	*Nassarius*	*Saccostrea*	*Tegillarca*	*Cymbiola*	*Volegalea*	*Modiolus*		*Telescopium*	*Geloina*	*Terebralia*	*Nerita*	
									Total					**Total**
NISP	1482	29	8	7	2	1	1	1	**1531**	3	2	2	1	**8**
MNI	741	15	8	4	2	1	1	1	**773**	3	2	2	1	**8**
Wt (g)	501.1	44.8	8.5	34.5	24.5	5.3	4.8	1.4	**624.9**	113.7	4.5	2.4	1.3	**121.9**

Results

The sample was dominated by *Mactra abbreviata* (Mytilidae, a marine species) (Table 3.19).

Yuluk a-jirrapa Mounds 1974

Yuluk a-jirrapa contains an impressive series of shell mounds, 1 km inland, adjacent to the home base of *Ngarli ji-bama*, on the eastern side of *An-gartcha Wana* (Map 3.1). The *An-barra* say they were formed by the large stingray *Yuluk*, who made these mounds as he flapped his way along the dune (Meehan 1982a, 167–8). The mound that was sampled was 24 m in diameter and 1.5 m high.

Sampling

Rhys took a sample at a depth of 10–15 cm.

Chronology

A *Dosinia juvenilis*/charcoal pair (ANU-2023) was dated to 636–165 and 240–23 cal BP respectively (Table 3.1).

Results

The dominant shellfish at *Yuluk a-jirrapa* was *Coecella horsfieldii*, a marine bivalve species found in intertidal coarse sand (Table 3.20; Meehan 1982a, 168).

Table 3.20. *Yuluk a-jirrapa* Shellfish taxa (% MNI).

	Coecella horsfieldii	*Dosinia*	*Mytilidae* (various)	*Mactra*	Other
% MNI	83	10	3	1.5	3

4
DISCUSSION AND CONCLUSION

Main archaeological site types on *An-barra* land

Given the lack of rock shelters, the main archaeological site types on *An-barra* land are all open. As mentioned in Chapter 2, there are three main types: shell middens, shell mounds and earth mounds (*gun-gapula*). They are typical of other areas on the coastal plains across the Top End of northern Australia (Brockwell et al. 2011).

The sites date from approximately 3,700 years ago until recently. The establishment of sites follows the progradation of the landscape, similar to what occurs in Blue Mud Bay (Faulkner 2013), but not for shell mounds in the Weipa area where coastal progradation slowed during the late Holocene (Shiner et al. 2013) and there does not seem to be a link between site age and distance to the coast (Holdaway et al. 2017; Morrison 2015). On *An-barra* territory, as described earlier, older sites, like *Mu-garnbal*, are located inland, while more recent sites, like *Guna-jengga* and *Jurnaka*, are located on the current coast (Map 3.1).

As well as following the evolution of the landscape, the faunal assemblages of these sites reflect change over time. As shellfish inhabit specific ecosystems, they are useful indicators of past environmental conditions and subsistence strategies. A change in species indicates a change in environment. For example, a shift from marine to estuarine species reflects a change in exploitation strategies focused on the sea to the mangroves and estuary of *An-gartcha Wana*.

Shell middens

The oldest site on *An-barra* land investigated so far is *Mu-garnbal*, a shell midden dated to c. 3,700 years BP (Table 3.1). It is in *Martay* territory on the eastern side of *An-gartcha Wana*, approximately 7 km from the coast (Map 3.1). Rhys compared *Mu-garnbal* with one of the modern-day coastal sites: "This is an inland outstation for the wet season and is in real contrast to the coastal strand loopers of *Lalarrgadjirripa*. Fascinating to hear that they are camped on a *gun-gapila* [mound]. I must go and see" (RJ FN 1973, Bk 14, 73).

Without knowing their age, Betty commented on the differences between the shell assemblages at *Mu-garnbal* and those on the coast:

> A sample taken from this site reflected its surroundings and contrasted with the… coastal middens… the main species being: *Anadara* [now *Tegillarca*] *granosa* (79%), *Cerithidea anticipata* (8%), *Telescopium telescopium* (6%), *Terebralia palustris* (4%), rest (6%)… The presence of mangrove species rarely used by the *Anbarra* is an important feature of these percentages. The large contribution of *Anadara* [*Tegillarca*] *granosa* also contrasted with *Anbarra* predation. *Tapes* [*Marcia*] *hiantina* was not recorded in the sample (Meehan 1982a, 167).

The dominance of *T. granosa*, a marine species, at *Mu-garnbal* (3,724–3,345 cal BP) is consistent with the site being close to the former coastline prior to progradation. This is also consistent with other *T. granosa* dominated sites across northern Australia at this time from northern Western Australia across the Top End to far north Queensland (see discussion on change over time below).

The other middens analysed for this study are younger. They date between 1,392 cal BP and recent, in descending chronological order:

- *Lorrkon a-jirrapa* (1,433–1,046 cal BP)
- *Muyu a-jirrapa* (1,392–987 cal BP)
- *Jilangga a-jirra* (1,235–703 cal BP)
- *Agajang-guwa* (1,060–683 cal BP)
- *Jinawunya* (740–430 cal BP)
- *Aningarra*'s Camp (515–30 cal BP)
- *Guna-jengga* (495–0 cal BP)
- *Jurnaka* (373–14 cal BP); and
- *Ngarli ji-bama* (286–0 cal BP) (Table 3.1).

These middens were dominated by species different from the ones Betty observed the *An-barra* collecting. In all cases, *Dosinia* was the dominant shellfish, except for the youngest site, *Ngarli ji-bama*, which was dominated by *Mactra* (Tables 3.8 and 3.19). These middens reflect a pattern of foraging from an environment different, though still marine based, from that observed by Betty in the 1970s, when the dominant shellfish collected was *Marcia hiantina* (see discussion below) and *Modiolus modulaides* from the home base at *Ngarli ji-bama*. There is a similar diversity of shellfish species in both shell mounds and middens.

Shell mounds

The shell mounds are dated between 1,356 cal BP and recently. In descending chronological order, they are *Muyu a-jirrapa* (1,356–867 cal BP), *Gulukula* (875–465 cal BP) and *Yuluk a-jirrapa* (636–165 cal BP) (Table 3.1). As stated in the last chapter, the contents of the *Muyu a-jirrapa* Shell Mound excavation were never analysed as the assemblage was lost in the Canberra bushfires of 2003. However, Rhys' observation from his 1974 samples was that the mound was dominated by *Dosinia* (RJ 1974, FN Bk 1, 90). *Gulukula* was also dominated by *Dosinia* (Table 3.4) and *Yuluk a-jirrapa* by *Coecella horsfieldii* (Table 3.20). Again, the assemblages of these shell mounds reflect shell foraging strategies from a variety of marine environments different from those that prevail at the sites today.

The date of 1,356–867 cal BP for *Muya A-jirripa* Shell Mound makes it contemporary with *Muya A-jirripa* Coastal Shell Midden (1,392–987 cal BP) (Table 3.1). Therefore, the fact that *Dosinia* is the dominant shellfish in both *Muya A-jirripa* Shell Mound and Coastal Shell Midden suggests that occupants of both sites were foraging from the same resource base (see previous chapter).

Earth mounds

Although there are numerous earth mounds located on the *An-gartcha Wana* floodplains, *Ji-bena* (1,284–790 cal BP) was the only one that was excavated, and an auger sample was taken from *Anamanba* (796–423 cal BP). The *Ji-bena* assemblage reflects a change in environmental conditions and exploitation strategies on the *An-gartcha Wana* floodplains. As *Ji-bena* is well dated archaeologically, these changes can be related to environmental shifts indicated by the floodplain's geomorphology, which have also been dated (see Chapter 2). *Ji-bena* also had the widest range of archaeological remains of all the sites excavated.

The assemblage was dominated by both marine and estuarine shellfish. There were also other faunal material and some stone artefacts (Table 3.7). Over time, the faunal remains indicate that a variety of different environments were being targeted from *Ji-bena* (Figure 3.14). Shellfish record the foraging in open beaches and mangrove environments. *Chelodina rugosa* (known as "long-necked turtle" in the Top End), northern brushtail possum (*Trichosurus arnhemensis*) and northern brown bandicoot (*Isoodon macrourus*), mark the exploitation of both freshwater swamps and open woodlands (Goodfellow 1993, 48).

Ji-bena now lies 8 km inland and the presence of marine shellfish in its assemblage suggests that the *Ji-bena* started life as a shell mound, perhaps when the coast was closer. *Dosinia juvenilis* dominated the shellfish assemblage from c. 1,300 years BP, immediately post the establishment of the mound until 988–609 cal BP (spit 8), when exploitation of this species declined and subsequently disappeared (Figure 3.12). Although they are far fewer in number, other marine species follow much the same pattern but did not disappear altogether. The foraging focus subsequently switched to mangrove shellfish, predominantly *Telescopium*. While less frequent, they are, with a couple of exceptions, present throughout the history of the mound, peaking after 988–609 cal BP, when the marine species decline dramatically (Figure 3.12). However, they too decline post this peak, perhaps indicating a general reorganisation of foraging strategies away from *Ji-bena* onto the prograding coastline. Betty notes that *Telescopium* is a gastropod and, in general, the *An-barra* did not seem to like them – they mainly collected them when bivalves were scarce or hard to get.

There followed a period of abandonment, apart from some sporadic occupation, until 710–333 cal BP (spit 5) when it was reoccupied as an earth mound. At that time, there was an increase of freshwater turtle in the upper levels of *Ji-bena*. This new foraging strategy coincides with the emergence of freshwater conditions in *Balpilja* close to the site, where the focus was now on freshwater produce from the swamp (Table 3.10, Figure 3.14).

The sample of *Geloina coaxans* (mangrove mud whelk) augered from 2.3 m below the surface of nearby *Anamanba* earth mound (Map 3.1) was dated to 796–423 cal BP (Table 3.1). This date overlaps with the decline of marine shellfish and the increase in mangrove species at *Ji-bena*, suggesting that *Anamanba* was occupied originally when the foraging focus had already shifted from marine to mangrove following environmental change associated with coastal progradation.

Stone assemblages

There is little stone suitable for knapping available on the coastal plains of *An-gartcha Wana*. The only stone quarry in *Gu-jingarliya* country is *Lawuk a-jirrapa* (stone-spear-point-place), a low rocky ridge on the western edge of the *An-barra* home base of *Ngarli ji-bama* (Figure 2.1, Map 3.1; Meehan 1982a, 26–7; Meehan & Jones 2005). *Ji-bena* is the only archaeological site that contains stone artefacts, mainly in its upper levels (Table 3.11, Figure 3.15). Apart from the quartzite artefacts, which were probably sourced locally from *Lawuk a-jirrapa*, the ground artefacts made from ochre, haematite and sandstone must have been traded in, possibly from sources in *Gun-nartpa* country to the south (Table 3.12). The lack of stone is notable as it emphasises *An-barra* reliance on ephemeral raw materials (bone, shell and wood) for their material culture, which was elaborate and multi-faceted (Meehan & Jones 2005). Betty recorded and collected many such items on her visits. This ethnographic collection is now housed in the MAGNT in Darwin.

The *An-barra* view

"Dead men"

The *An-barra* make a distinction between shell middens and shell mounds. Betty commented:

> While walking through the bush *Anbarra* people often commented about a specific site, describing its place in the annual cycle and naming the people who had camped there as well as what they would have eaten. Thus, some sites are designated 'cold weather camps', others 'rain-time camps', and so on. When people cannot name the people who inhabited a particular site, they usually attribute it to 'dead men', meaning that it was inhabited by *Gidjingali* ancestors whose names they cannot, or do not want, to remember (Meehan 1982a, 166).

In this context, Rhys commented about *Guna-jengga* as a remembered *rrawa*, that is, recognised as a camp site not a Dreaming (RJ FN 1973, Bk 23, 3–4). Betty also explained: "The structure of all midden deposits attributed to 'dead men' are consistent with contemporary *Anbarra* customs. In fact, the important home base sites of *Ngalidjibama* and *Kopanga* are located on areas containing extensive non-continuous midden deposits" (Meehan 1982a, 166–7).

"Dreamings"

About the shell mounds, Betty said: "These have an obvious human origin, but the *Anbarra* say they are not the work of man but of the 'Dreaming'. The mounds do not occur on the coast but inland at least 1 km on a series of fossil dunes. They are found on both sides of the river in *Anbarra*, *Gulala* and *Matai* territory" (Meehan 1982a, 167). Here, this especially relates to the *Gulukula* and *Yuluk a-jirrapa* shell mounds, both of which are Dreaming places.

> The relationship between contemporary *Anbarra* customs, 'dead men' sites and 'Dreaming' is one of the intriguing problems in the prehistory of the Blyth River area. In the contemporary diet *Tapes hiantina* [*Marcia hiantina*] is the dominant species. In the *Anbarra* 'dead men' sites the contribution of this species [is] below 14%. While in the *Kula Kula* mound it formed but 2% of the shell sample. Conversely, *Dosinia juvenilis*, which was relatively unimportant in 1972–73 (0.4%), comprised 91% of the shells in this last sample (Meehan1982a, 168).

Again, these observations are supported by the archaeological analysis in the previous chapter.

> In terms of structure, the 1972–73 *An-barra* and 'dead men' camps extending along the beach front dunes and leaving extensive intermittent deposits are basically the same, but both differ markedly from the 'Dreaming' mounds which imply isolated, confined camping areas. From their geomorphological positions and the fact that they are no longer remembered as the camps of men, we believe that the 'Dreaming' mounds are considerably older than the 'dead' men sites and are related to the exploitation of a coastline that is different from the present one. Shell mounds similar in size and shape are situated both to the west at Maningrida and to the east at Milingimbi [Map 1.1] and on the *Ngan-galala* plains, to say nothing of the Weipa and other mounds further afield in Cape York, Queensland. The *Gidjingali* 'Dreaming' mounds may thus belong to this broader class of sites whose ecological and social contexts are not yet fully understood (Meehan 1982a, 168).

Despite Betty and Rhys' thoughts about the older age of the shell mounds, the radiocarbon chronology established that they are contemporary with the shell middens, the shell midden at *Mu-garnbal* being by far the oldest site on *An-barra* land. So, age does not determine whether the *An-barra* classify sites as belonging to "dead men" or the "Dreaming"; rather, it is the foraging behaviour that created the sites in the first place. The *An-barra* recognise middens as belonging to people because they still create such sites themselves today, while the shell mounds are the result of foraging strategies from the past that are no longer familiar, hence they were created by mythical beings from the Dreaming (for further discussion, see Brockwell 2013).

Archaeological change over time: *An-gartcha Wana*

The archaeology on *An-barra* land reflects the changing landscape over the last 3,700 years. The establishment of the sites follows the progradation of the landscape, with the older sites, like *Mu-garnbal* located inland, to more recent sites, like *Guna-jengga* and *Jinawunya* located on the current coast. The predominance of *Tegillarca* (a marine species) at *Mu-garnbal* reflects the time when the site was located adjacent to the seashore before the floodplains of *An-gartcha Wana* silted up, as discussed previously. Betty said of the change in diet over time,

> though I do not have detailed figures for their [*Matai*] shellfish consumption [at Maganbal] during 1972–73 I know that they at least ate shellfish of all

> the species represented with the addition of *Tapes* [*Marcia*] *hiantina* from *Lalarr-gadjirripa* and various species of Mytilidae from *Moganarra*. As for the *Anbarra*, *Tapes* [*Marcia*] *hiantina* have become more important for the *Matai* in recent times (1982, 166–7).

The cheniers adjacent to the coast at *Jinawunya* (1,264–887 cal BP) and *Gulukula* (1,150–750 cal BP) are the most recent. The archaeological sites of the same names are dated to 875–465 cal BP (*Gulukula*) and 740–430 cal BP (*Jinawunya*). The next chenier inland, *Lorrkon a-jirrapa*, has been dated to 1,839–1,355 cal BP, and its associated archaeological site to 1,433–1,046 cal BP (Table 3.1).

With increasing rainfall in the last 1,500 years, freshwater ponded behind the cheniers and large mangrove swamps became freshwater wetlands. Dating of faunal assemblages from *Ji-bena* shows that *Balpilja* Swamp was freshwater from at least 700 years ago and probably as early as 1,000 years BP (Figure 3.14; Brockwell 2013; Chappell & Jones 1999; Thurtell et al. 1999). These dates emphasise the recent nature of the current *An-gartcha Wana* landscape.

Continuity

Despite these changes, Betty and Rhys constantly emphasise the continuity in the traditions between the archaeological sites and present-day camps: "In no prehistoric site did I notice any species that were not eaten at some time during 1972–73, but the relative importance of some species was markedly different in these old sites" (Meehan 1982a, 168).

> The 'dead men' sites represent both continuity with, and contrast between, contemporary *Gidjingali* practices. The structures of the sites are consistent with modern *Anbarra* behaviour, the species of shellfish eaten also being the same. The contrast is in the relative importance of these species. In 1972–73 *Tapes* [*Marcia*] *hiantina* were collected far more frequently than any other species contributing 61% of the gross weight of all shellfish collected during the year. For people living at the *Kopanga* [*Aningarra*'s Camp] and *Gunadjang-ga* 'dead men' sites this species contributes merely 14% and 3% respectively. *Dosinia juvenilis* taking its place at both sites and contributing 33% and 60% respectively (Meehan 1982a, 167).

This observation is supported by the analysis of the shell middens in the previous chapter.

Rhys reflected on the *Guna-jengga* archaeological site:

> The interesting thing is that the 'dinner time camp' associated with the fish trap – i.e. the one under the 2 bushes on the dune – is in line with the middle and is stratigraphically just slightly above it – or the same level. Thus we have a 'recent' but 'prehistoric' midden – and one from the ethnographic present being found in the same place and for the same purpose – the old traditions and camp site use continued to the observed present – e.g. the little hearth and midden – deposited a week or two ago (RJ FN 1973, Bk 21, 27).

Both Betty and Rhys note that a modern hearth overlies the existing midden at *Muyu a-jirrapa*: "About 4.30 pm we went to some work on the eroding dune (coastal midden) at *Miadjirripa*. It is about 12" thick and comes almost to the present-day surface. Right on top of this midden there was a 'recent' hearth with crab, fish and *angalidjauwurigia* remains visible in it" (BM FN 1974 Bk 1, 90). Rhys commented: "Thus, the modern activity is located directly above the older midden, and its debris (of modern activity) forming its uppermost component" (RJ 1974 FN, Bk 1, 84).

Rhys reflected:

> I felt here, walking over the middens, that even if I could not get permission to dig at one, it did not really matter – the unique and important factor here, was that this was one of the few places in Australia (or the world for that matter) where hunters are still intimately tied to their landscape and to that of their distant forebears. Must get a date for the top of the midden – to give a value to the time it takes for H/G culture to forget an old camping ground. F.G. also said that when people want to camp on the middens – the *Kula Kula* tends to press them away… 'Kula Kula shift 'im' (RJ 1972 FN, Bk 9, 19–20).

Archaeological change over time: The bigger picture

The onset of the Holocene climatic optimum (9,000–6,000 years BP) coincided with rapid expansion of populations and establishment of new sites across much of Australia. Williams et al. (2015) argue that more favourable environmental conditions at the end of this period allowed longer periods of residence, resulting in a shift to more sedentary lifestyles in some parts of the continent.

Williams et al. (2015) argue that, despite highly variable climates, over the last 6,000 years in Australia, the increased number of radiocarbon dates from archaeological sites in this period suggests increasing population. After sea-level stabilisation c. 6,000 years ago, sedimentation from rivers filled coastal embayments creating ideal shallow-water conditions for shellfish beds. During that time, there was increased exploitation of coastal resources along the northern and eastern coastlines with sites being mainly shell mounds or middens. Building of conical shell mounds (mainly of *Tegillarca* but also of other species like *Dosinia* and *Marcia*) occurred across northern Australia from c. 4,000 years BP, including Queensland and Western Australia (Clune & Harrison 2009; Cochrane 2014; Harrison 2009; Holdaway et al. 2017; O'Connor 1999; Shiner et al. 2013; Veitch 1999). In the Top End of Australia, the construction of shell mounds ceased abruptly c. 500 years ago (Brockwell et al. 2009). However, it seems they may have continued into more recent times on the Weipa Peninsula in western Cape York, where Morrison (2013, 2014, 2015) argues shell mound building persisted until contact, and on the Abydos Plain in Western Australia (Clune & Harrison 2009; Harrison 2009).

Researchers suggest that changes in *Tegillarca* habitats around 800 to 500 years ago contributed to a notable ecological shift from open beach and mudflats to the mangrove-rich environments seen along much of the coastline today (Bourke 2012; Faulkner 2013; Hiscock 1997). Evidence from the earth mound at *Ji-bena* suggests similar environmental transformations occurred along the Blyth River during this period (Brockwell et al. 2005). Furthermore, there is widespread documentation of social and economic adaptations across northern Australia at that time. For example, Brockwell (2009) highlights changes in faunal and stone tool assemblages in earth mounds along the floodplains of the lower Adelaide River 600 years ago. In the Torres Strait, significant transformations in demographics, mobility, rituals, seascape construction, social ties and exchange practices are noted between 800 and 600 years ago, as well as between 500 and 400 years ago (Barham et al. 2004, 37; David & Badulgal 2006; McNiven 2006, 9–10). In north Queensland, David and Wilson (1999) describe *Ngarrabullgan,* a mountain now regarded as ritually dangerous and avoided by traditional custodians, which bears evidence of substantial occupation before 600 years cal BP (Hiscock 2008, 274–5; Hiscock & Faulkner 2006, 219–20).

Bourke et al. (2007) suggest that major climatic shifts between 800 and 500 years ago caused environmental change that led to these shifts in economic and cultural practices around Darwin. Isotope analysis of shell samples taken from Darwin Harbour, *An-gartcha Wana*, and Blue Mud Bay in eastern Arnhem Land show widespread shifts in sea surface temperatures throughout the region at this time (Brockwell et al. 2013).

Influence of the Vanuatu volcano?

Evidence of a possible causal factor for economic and social change in the late Holocene in northern Australia comes from Kuwae in Vanuatu, where there was a major volcanic eruption in the 1450s CE. It was one of the largest volcanic eruptions recorded, profoundly influencing not just the immediate area in Vanuatu but also extending its effects worldwide. Locally, the eruption devastated the former island of Kuwae, leaving behind the islands of Tongoa and Epi, which significantly reshaped the political, linguistic and ecological landscapes of central Vanuatu (Ballard et al. 2023).

On a global scale, the Kuwae eruption is often linked to the onset of the Little Ice Age (c. 1,450–1,530 CE) in the Northern Hemisphere that led to economic hardships across various regions. Current research being conducted at ANU by Stuart Bedford and Chris Ballard seeks to verify both the timing and magnitude of the eruption at its source, located on the islands of Epi and Tongoa (Culture, History and Language 2024). This data may shed light on the chronology of late Holocene environmental change and changes in Aboriginal economic and social strategies in northern Australia.

Ethnographic analogy

In 1988, Betty Meehan and Rhys Jones published an edited volume, *Archaeology with Ethnography: An Australian Perspective*, based on papers presented at the 1983 AAA conference on the same theme. Their main motivation for this publication was their reaction against the processualists who at that time argued a purist view that "archaeology, to be a respectable and autonomous discipline, must be capable of carrying out its entire intellectual processes within its own terms and with no derivation of core ideas from cognate disciplines" (Meehan & Jones 1988, viii).

There were some seminal papers presented in this volume, which are still widely quoted. Meehan (1982a) based her information on her long periods of fieldwork with the *An-barra* people of the *An-gartcha Wana* in the 1970s. She defined "dinner time camps" as "small campsites used during the day while people are engaged in hunting trips away from their home bases where people cook and eat food that has been procured up to that time" (Meehan 1982a, 26; 1988b). She argued that dinner time camps could be distinguished archaeologically as mainly being small in size and containing monospecific faunal remains, whereas base camps are larger and much more varied in their assemblages.

More recently, there has been renewed interest in and debate about archaeology using ethnography as an interpretive tool, with an increasing commitment to community archaeology and Indigenous-driven research projects (e.g. Allen &

Rowe 2014; Clarke 2002; David et al. 2021, 2024; Guilfoyle et al. 2013; Hiscock 2013; Hiscock & Faulkner 2006; Holdaway & Allen 2011; MacFarlane et al. 2005; McNiven 2016; Molle et al. 2023; Morrison 2014; Ross et al. 2013; Thomas et al. 2023; Urwin et al. 2024; Wright et al. 2021).

Several authors propose that the "ethnographic present" began at least 500 years ago in coastal northern Australia (e.g. Brockwell 2013; David & Badulgal 2006; David & Weisler 2006; David & Wilson 1999; Hiscock 2013; Hiscock & Faulkner 2006; McNiven 2006), with major changes to previous environments, and Indigenous economies from that time onwards similar to those recorded in the Contact period. The importance of this argument is that ethnographic analogy then becomes a valid tool in archaeological interpretation of the past over the last 500 years.

Hiscock and Faulkner (2006) explore the formation of shell mounds along the northern coastal plains, drawing on ethnographic analogy and mythology. Researchers (e.g. Bourke 2005; Clune & Harrison 2009; Cribb 1996; Morrison 2003; Veitch 1999) have relied on ethnographic insights to decode the origins as well as the ritualistic and social aspects of these mounds. However, Hiscock and Faulkner assert: "Attempts to impose historic ideologies and cosmologies on earlier times fail to acknowledge the magnitude and rate of economic and ideological change on the tropical coastline of Australia" (2006, 209). Their argument suggests that between 3,000 and 500 years ago, before shell mound construction halted, foragers operated in a landscape that differed significantly from what we see today. Moreover, the fact that many existing shell mounds now sit in barren, unproductive areas has led many Aboriginal communities to perceive them not as human-made structures, but rather as natural formations or as creations of their "Dreaming" ancestors. Consequently, Hiscock (2008, 272–5) and Hiscock and Faulkner (2006, 216) contend that employing modern ethnographic comparisons is inadequate for understanding shell mounds. They suggest that

> historically recorded understandings of the mounds probably emerged only after the termination of the economic and environmental system that created them, as these relic structures were conceptualised by people with transformed economies and views about the land. During the last 800–600 years, the myths about and uses of these sites came to reflect the concerns, perceptions and ideology of historic and proto-historic Aboriginal people (Hiscock & Faulkner, 2006, 217).

The shell mound "Dreamings", *Yuluk a-jirrapa* and *Gulukula*, both on *An-barra* territory, demonstrate that such is the case. However, the shell middens there also represent relics from a transformed landscape but they are recognised by the *An-barra* as being humanly constructed "dead men" sites, even though *Mu-garnbal* is dated to 3,500 years ago. This implies that the situation is more complex than Hiscock and Faulkner have argued as the *An-barra* today have insight into settlement patterns of previous landscapes. This indicates the value of ethnographic analogy and Indigenous explanations to interpret local archaeological sites dated to the late Holocene.

Linguistic evidence

Margaret Carew (pers. comm. 18 July 2024), the linguist who assisted in the translation of Betty's text "For the *An-barra*" into *Gu-jingarliya* (see following chapter) noted that:

> The group name *An-barra* has long been translated into English as "people of the rivermouth" (cf. Gurrmanamana et al. 2002). This name is built on the body part word *barra*. It sounds the same but has a different meaning from *barra* "monsoon wind" and is a different part of speech in grammatical terms.
>
> There is a class of words in *Burarra* that are "shape classifiers" (e.g. *barra* "base part", *jawa* "throat", *bama* "head", *gochila* "belly" etc.). These words are often derived into other words, where the semantics of shape and part/whole relations are relevant. For example, *jin-gochila* is a word built on *gochila* "belly", and means "mother" or "mother's clan group" (derived by adding the female prefix *jin-* onto the base word). *An-barra* is a word built on *barra* "bottom, underneath part". We get this by adding the masculine prefix *an-* onto the base word barra (*an-* can also agree with a group of people). It literally means "people associated with something that is underneath".
>
> As a body part or shape classifier word, *barra* refers to the bottom of something and also the underneath or submerged part of something. For example, *barra gu-jirra* "the depths of a billabong", and *gu-barra* "in the deep water" are some of the constructions with this term where the "underwater" meaning is evident.
>
> It was curious why *barra* is recruited for "rivermouth", given that another body part *jawa* "throat" is more commonly used for this part of a river. From reading Betty and Rhys' work, as well as that of anthropologist Geoff Bagshaw, it was realised that *An-barra*, as a group name, refers to the fact

> that these people own country that is submerged by the sea and includes sites in the rivermouth of *An-gartcha Wana*.

As indicated previously, the *An-barra* have an intimate knowledge of their landscape and are acutely aware of changes over time. The meaning of *An-barra* demonstrates that knowledge.

In eastern Arnhem Land, a multi-disciplinary study using geomorphology, archaeology, anthropology and linguistics determined that toponyms from Yolngu country around Blue Mud Bay (Map 1.1) were established up to 3,000 years ago and that the current social system may have considerable time depth (Morphy et al. 2020). This may also be the case with *An-barra* territory.

Genetic evidence

White and Parsons (1973, 1976) carried out population genetics research in Arnhem Land in the 1970s that is relevant to *An-barra* history in that area. White provided a summary of his relevant findings below:

> … using fingerprints and some other single-gene characters, the four small language groups around Maningrida, including the Anbarra or Burarra, are distinctive and can be distinguished from other surrounding populations. As they are genetically distinguishable, so too are they by language. Linguists have shown that these groups belong to four language families, the highest level of language differentiation in Australia. The fact that there is little genetic differentiation within this small cluster indicates that there was intermarriage across the language family boundaries but not inland. The fingerprint characters, particularly total ridge count, help resolve the relationship of the Yolngu of northeast Arnhem Land to the Burarra. The latter have been considered by some to belong to the Yolngu complex. However, it is clear from [this] study that there is marked genetic differentiation between the two, when the Yolgnu are considered as a whole, suggesting reproductive isolation over a significant period of time, or different origins. The genetic results also suggest that the Anbarra with their immediate neighbours have differentiated genetically either through reproductive isolation, that is, highly localised marriage distances over many generations with evidence of very limited marriages away from the coast, or demographically unstable small populations, that is numbers have fluctuated markedly through time, although it is possible that both these mechanisms have operated across many generations. Certainly, the very favourable subsistence base, with access to both marine and terrestrial (plants and animals) resources, provides opportunity for population stability through

sufficient time to generate both the observed linguistic and population genetic difference in this part of coastal Arnhem Land (pers. comm. 2023).

Conclusion

The *An-barra* Archaeological Project aimed to explore pre-colonial settlement and subsistence patterns in central Arnhem Land, considering the significant environmental changes on northern Australia's coastal plains during the mid to late Holocene. Additionally, the archaeological findings were analysed alongside ethnographic insights from Betty's book, *Shell Bed to Shell Midden* (Meehan 1982a), highlighting both connections and disparities while seeking to understand the underlying reasons.

The site types on *An-barra* territory – shell mounds, shell middens and earth mounds – are typical of other areas on the coastal plains across the Top End of northern Australia. The earliest site so far recorded, *Mu-garnbal*, dated to 3,700 years, is located inland close to the palaeo-estuary of *An-gartcha Wana*. Establishment of sites generally over the next few thousand years followed the evolution and progradation of the landscape with the younger ones closest to the present-day coast.

Like the archaeological record from other regions in late Holocene northern Australia, *Ji-bena* records major changes in *An-barra* subsistence patterns c. 800–500 years ago suggesting major environmental change at that time. A possible causal factor is the massive volcanic eruption in Kuwae, Vanuatu, c. 1,450 CE, which would have disrupted climate and sea surface temperatures, creating new environments.

Change and continuity are both themes of the research. Foraging patterns recorded by Betty and Rhys in the 1970s differ from those found archaeologically, in terms of shellfish species harvested. Settlement patterns differ in that large conical shell mounds are no longer created and low, diffuse shell middens are the more recent archaeological expression. Despite changes in foraging behaviour, the shellfish species eaten today are the same as those eaten in the past, just the proportions differ, and "dead men" sites are similar to shell middens today and recognised by the *An-barra* as such.

The ethnographic and linguistic evidence indicates that the *An-barra* are well aware of changes over time to their landscape. Despite its recent nature, it is covered in place names emphasising *An-barra* adaptability and the continuity of their social traditions in the face of change. Continuity is also emphasised by the evidence of genetic differentiation from neighbouring groups that suggests highly localised marriage over many generations. In conclusion, ethnography and Aboriginal world views can add depth and detail to previous lifeways that archaeology cannot, and both complement and enrich archaeological interpretation.

5

FOR THE *AN-BARRA*: TEXT IN ENGLISH (BETTY MEEHAN)

Note [from the Glasgow (1994) dictionary]

> *-guwarr* (p. 343): "old customs and culture from before the white man; traditional; of long ago".
>
> *gun-guwarr* (p. 318): … See *-guwarr*. The prefix "*gun*" probably describes an old place from before the arrival of white people (Betty Meehan, pers. comm. 14 August 2024).

I am Betty Meehan, and this is a story about *An-barra* history. Les Hiatt and I came to Maningrida in 1958. We came from Canberra, a long way from *An-barra* country. We flew from Canberra to Darwin on an aeroplane (Map 5.1). After that we went from Darwin to Maningrida on a boat. The boat belonged to Curly Bell, and it was called *The Kaprys*. The sea was rough when we travelled.

When we arrived, we saw your old people living in Maningrida, on *Kunibidji* country. They were far from their country at *An-gartcha Wana*. They lived in a different way to *balanda*.

Les said to them, "I want to learn about how you live, about language, kinship and other things." Les and I said, "We will build our tent here." Some *An-barra* men helped us. We said, "The earth is dusty, let's put shells on the ground inside the tent." From our tent, we looked north towards where the northwest monsoon blows from, we faced the beautiful Maningrida beach to Boucaut Bay and, in the distance, the Arafura Sea.

When *Barra* came, we put up another tent. Then we had more shelter from *Barra* winds from the northwest. The *Barra* winds are strong. The new tent was big and we had more room to talk to *An-barra* people.

Map 5.1. Maningrida, NT to Canberra, ACT (map data © 2025 Google, annotated by Adam Black).

Figure 5.1. Betty collecting shellfish early in the wet season of 1973 (Rhys Jones).

Figure 5.2. Students attending Maningrida School 1958 (Betty Meehan).

It was really good to sit and talk with everyone. Les soon made friends with several senior *An-barra* men (including Les A. and Frank G.) They visited him regularly. They began to tell him about *An-barra* language, kinship systems, marriage rules, religion and the right path to follow in life.

As they talked, I looked after everyone. I gave Les and the men food and drink. I also spent time with *An-barra* young mums with their kids and older women. We all went hunting together out bush, collecting shellfish, fish and long yams (Figure 5.1).

An important man, Dr Herbert Cole "Nugget" Coombs (Governor of the Reserve Bank of Australia), visited Maningrida while Les and I were there, in 1958. He said to me, "Hey, why don't you start a school?" I set up the first school at Maningrida

(Figure 5.2). Several *An-barra* children (for example, Sam G.) were part of my first class of about 20 children – 10 girls and 10 boys. This small school has grown into a large and flourishing high school, which celebrated its 60th anniversary in 2018.

Les and I lived at Maningrida for one year. After that, Les and I returned to Canberra. Les thought about all the wonderful stories the *An-barra* men had explained to him. He wrote down all these stories. I worked as a teacher, teaching small children in Ainslie Public School.

In 1960, we came back to Maningrida. Les resumed his conversations with *An-barra* people. This time, we erected our tent away from the coast. We sheltered from the strong wind and rain during the wet season. I continued to spend time with *An-barra* women and children. The small school that I had established in 1958 had grown into a thriving establishment with highly dedicated teachers and lessons being carried out in some of the local Aboriginal languages.

I wanted to learn more about the food that *An-barra* people ate. I wanted to learn how they collected and prepared different foods, such as cycads, water chestnuts, *Ipomoea* yams, long yams, lily roots, Venus cockles, mangrove worms, mussels, and everything like that. I wanted to learn about dillybags, digging sticks, the firewood used to cook long-necked turtles, how to cook with termite mound, and so I learned all about this as I went along.

During the two years that Les and I lived at Maningrida (1958, 1960), we made some trips into the surrounding countryside, walking along the high ground and along the coastline. Les walked a few times to *An-barra* country guided by senior *An-barra* men so that they could show him important places. Together we made one trip to *Balpilja* Swamp with a small group of people (*Balanda* [white man] and Aboriginal). Dr Stuart Scougall and Dorothy Bennett (Figure 5.3) came with us. Stuart and Dorothy wanted to learn about the beautiful bark paintings that Aboriginal artists were painting at Maningrida. Another time, we walked along the beach with some *An-barra* owners. We walked from Maningrida to *An-gartcha Wana*. We camped for a few days at *Gupanga*. Then we came back.

Just before we left Maningrida in 1960, Nancy Bandeiyama gave birth to a baby girl – Betty Ngurrpangurrpa (Figure 5.4). As she grew up, she became a dear friend and continues to educate me about *An-barra* life until the present day – sometimes by mobile phone!

Some of you first met Rhys Jones in 1972. Rhys has passed away now. He came with me to live with you at *Gupanga*, *Lalarr Gu-jirrapa* and some other places on *An-barra* country. Rhys was an archaeologist. He wanted to learn about how home bases (*rrawa*) had been occupied by *An-barra* people for a long time in the past.

Figure 5.3. Left to right: Three unidentified individuals, art collector Dorothy Bennett, Les Hiatt and Betty Meehan [formerly Hiatt] (Betty Meehan).

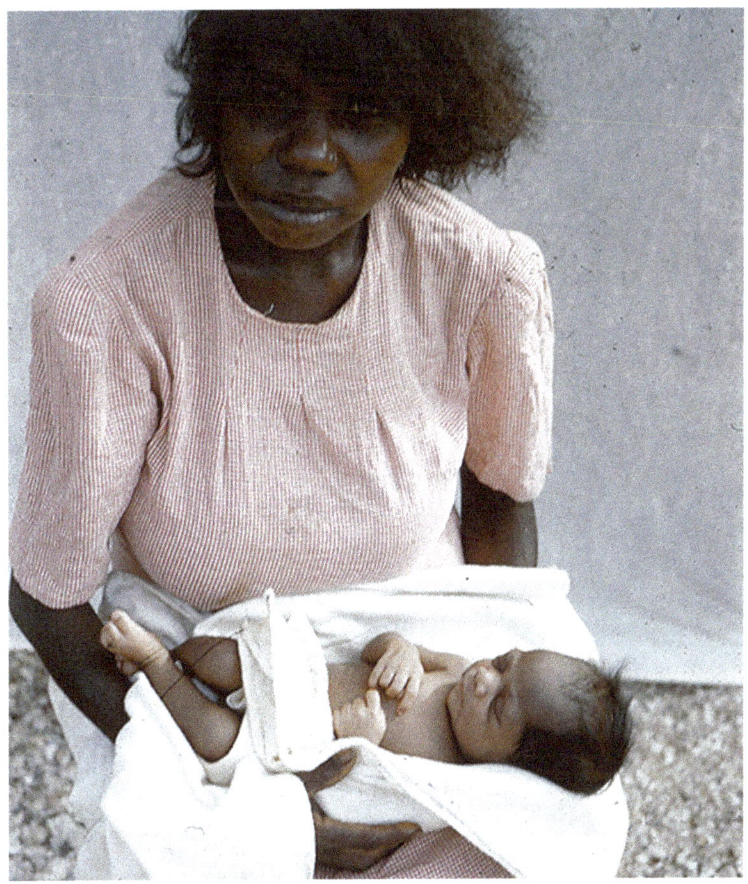

Figure 5.4. Nancy Bandieyama with Betty Ngurrpangurrpa as a baby 1960 (Betty Meehan).

During the time we spent with the *An-barra* over the years (1972 to the present), we were shown many *rrawa* where living and deceased *An-barra* people had lived in the past. They also showed us and told stories about some places that are part of the Dreaming. Most of these sites contained some shellfish, animal bones, charcoal and, sometimes, some stone tools.

Scientists at ANU have used a radiocarbon dating machine to find out how old the animal remains are. To do this, they put small pieces of shell, bone or charcoal in the machine. Eventually, the machine produces answers that give some idea of how long ago Aboriginal people might have been living at the *rrawa* from which the samples came. Below, I will refer to this machine as the Dating Machine.

Rhys' last trip to *An-barra* country was in 1999. He came with John Chappell. Rhys and John worked with some *An-barra* people, Betty Ngurrpangurrpa, Elva Jindjerakama and Stewart Rankin. They collected shells, bones, charcoal and stones from many places on *An-barra* land. They wanted to find out when *An-barra* people or their ancestors lived there.

Over centuries of time, as you may well know, the sea next to the Arnhem Land coast has moved in and out – sometimes huge distances – and, probably, sometimes destroying camp sites and other features of human occupation. You can find a complete list of all the dates in Chapter 3.

Rhys died from leukaemia in Canberra Hospital in 2001. This was a year after the work he and John carried out. Betty Ngurrpangurrpa went to see Rhys in hospital before he died. John Chappell died in New Zealand in 2018. Sally Brockwell has continued to work with me so that we could finish the work that Rhys and I started many years ago.

Next, we describe some of the *rrawa* that Rhys and I recorded and for which we have been able to obtain some dates telling us how long ago these *rrawa* might have been used by *An-barra* and/or other Aboriginal people. You can find more information about all these *rrawa* in *Gun-guwarr*.

Aningarra's Camp

Aningarra's Camp lies to the north of where we were all living at *Gupanga* in 1972–73.

Michael Aningarra and his family were living on top of this site in 1972. The midden beneath contained the remains of shellfish from the sea and the mangroves – for example, *an-dirrbula* [*Dosinia*], *jina-guronggura* [*Mactra*] and *an-jiwirriga* [mussels], as well as charcoal from cooking fires. The Dating Machine at ANU told us that your old people were living here from about 300 years ago.

Gulukula mounds

As you know, these large mounds of shell are found on the western side of *An-gartcha Wana*. They are about one kilometre from the sea. Frank G. took me and Rhys to see them. He said they are Dreaming places belonging to *Gulukula* (dog). *Gulukula* piled up these mounds of shell with his paws.

Remains of shellfish from both the mangroves and the open sea were found in the site – mostly *an-dirrbula* but also some *an-juwurrgiya* and *jina-guronggura*. These shells were analysed by the Dating Machine, which showed that the old people visited this place about 900 years ago.

Guna-jengga rrawa

As you know, *Guna-jengga* is a coastal site where, most years, some of you installed a large *an-gujechiya* (fish trap) across the creek behind the first dune. Rhys and I have been there with you many times when you caught a big mob of fish and other sea food in the *an-gujechiya*. Once, when we were with you, you found a huge pile of turtle eggs buried on the beach!

Some *an-dirrbula* shells and charcoal from the *rrawa* were processed by the Dating Machine that told us that *Guna-jengga* has been used by people as far back as 500 years ago.

Gupanga wangarr an-dakal a-yurra (where the Dreaming white ochre representing *diyama* lies)

As you know, the *diyama* [*Marcia*] Dreaming place is located about 400 metres just north of *Gupanga rrawa*. Harry *Mulumbuk* and Barney *Girrirrwanga* sang a song about this site. Harry painted a bark painting depicting the *diyama* story. The Dating Machine has shown that this site is about 1,450 years old.

Ji-bena rrawa

I remember the day that Frank G. took Rhys and me to see the huge earth mound, *Ji-bena*, near *Balpilja* Swamp. On that day, he and other *An-barra* men with him, shot some wallabies and cooked them on the edge of the *Ji-bena* mound using some ant bed collected from nearby to cook them!

He described how, in the past, he and other *An-barra* people had visited this area when it was a good time to get ducks, geese and several types of plant food growing in the nearby swamps. He also described how, in the past, large groups of people had camped on top of these mounds to avoid the dampness on the plains, building shelters up there.

Some of you may also remember that when Rhys and I were carrying out our small excavation at *Ji-bena*, some *An-barra* people (e.g. Betty Ngurrpangurrpa) helped.

When we were digging, we found the remains of 19 different kinds of shellfish – but *an-dirrbula* was the most common. Bone fragments were also found in the excavation – mostly in the top levels – these were from turtles, mammals, fish (catfish and barramundi), reptiles and birds. Also, mostly in the top levels, we found some flaked stone tools, one bipolar stone core, some ground ochre and some artefacts made from haematite and sandstone. The Dating Machine shows that *Ji-bena* was first visited by the old people about 1,300 years ago.

Jilangga a-jirra

As you know, *Jilangga a-jirra* is a wet season *rrawa* located on the eastern side of *An-gartcha Wana* about two kilometres from the coast. When the airport at *Jimarda* was built, it was close to this camp, and people said, "This is too close to the airport, let's move down to the beach at *Yilan*."

Dates from *an-dirrbula* shells show that the old people were living at this place as far back as 1,200 years ago.

Jinawunya

As you know, *Jinawunya* is a *rrawa* on the western side of *An-gartcha Wana* where people went to collect shellfish, fish, *Pandanus* nuts, fibre for weaving, fruit and wood. A sample of *an-garlajawurrga* shows that people have been using this site for 700 years.

Jurnaka

This is the *Belanggil* area, near *Gupanga*. There is a mound there. The proper name is *Dar A-yurrapa* ("where the bamboo vine lies") The word *Jurnaka* means "corner", it's where the river turns and goes up toward *Gochan Jiny-jirra*. *Jurnaka* is in a mangrove area on the western side of the mouth of *An-gartcha Wana*.

When Rhys and I were living with you, people went to this place to catch fish, stingray and different kinds of shellfish, including oysters from the mangroves.

A sample of *an-dirrbula* processed in the Dating Machine shows that people were probably using this place from about 400 years ago.

Lorrkon a-jirrapa ("where the *lorrkon* stands")

As you know, *Lorrkon a-jirrapa* shell middens are located on the western side of *An-gartcha Wana.* Some stone flakes (tools) have been found on the ground at some of these sites. The *an-dirrbula* shells used in the Dating Machine show that these middens could be as old as about 1,400 years.

Mu-garnbal rrawa

As you know, this *rrawa*, which belongs to the *Martay* group, is situated on the eastern bank of *An-gartcha Wana* about 12 kilometres from the sea.

Rhys and I visited this place several times during our stays at *Gupanga.* I remember one day when we sailed there in that large dugout canoe called *Mu-garnbal* – with David B., Mary, Laurie and Jimmy.

The people there were hunting for native mice and goannas on the plain country. The mice live in the grass, and the goannas live in burrows. The goannas would all run out when they burnt the grass, and so would the native mice.

During the wet season, some *Martay* people camped at *Mu-garnbal* on top of a small shell midden. Shells from that midden, *ana-mula an-ika* [*Terebralia*], show that the old people lived at this *rrawa* about 3,700 years ago! This is the oldest archaeological site we have dated so far.

Muyu a-jirrapa ("where the fly stands")

This is a coastal site made up of a linear midden on the seaward side and a shell mound behind. By 1979, the midden was mostly destroyed by a very rough sea. A date from *an-dirrbula* shells shows that both the midden and the mound were used by the old people about 1,400 years ago.

Ngarli ji-bama

As you know, *Ngarli ji-bama* is a home base situated on an inland dune on the eastern side of *An-gartcha Wana.* People lived there during the dry season. Some shellfish that could be *jina-guronggura* suggest that people have been using this *rrawa* for about 300 years.

Yuluk a-jirrapa ("stingray stands there")

These shell mounds are located about one kilometre inland near *Ngarli ji-bama* home base – and are said to have been formed by the large stingray *Yuluk*. Some *an-dirrbula* shells and charcoal tell us that this place is about 600 years old.

FOR THE *AN-BARRA*: TEXT IN GU-JINGARLIYA

Gun-guwelamagapa: Gun-nerranga gun-nerranga rrawa, An-barra gun-nika

First translation 27 June 2024 Freda Wyartja and Doreen Jinggarrbarra

Checked 28 June 2024 Betty Ngurrpangurrpa and Elva Gindjerakama

Updated by Margaret Carew 4 July 2024 (Figure 5.5).

Ngaypa Betty Meehan, ngu-weya janguny, An-barra an-guwelamagapa gun-nika janguny mu-ngoyurra gun-guyinda.

Les rrapa ngaypa nyirri-bena 1958, Maningrida nyirri-dechinga. Nyirri-bawana Canberra bulaypulay.

Ngatipa Canberra wenga nyirri-garlmana, nyirri-rakija Darwin, arriplan mu-guyinda.

Gu-gata wenga gapala mu-guyinda Darwin nyirri-warrchinga.

Nyirri-bamana, Maningrida nyirri-bena.

Mun-guna gapala, Curly Bell mun-nika, mun-nelangga Kaprys.

Gun-bachirra bartpa wana gu-ni, nyirri-bamana gurda.

Nyirri-bena, nyirrbu-nana gapala yerrcha, aburr-ninya Kunibidji gun-nika rrawa.

Gun-gata gun-birripa rrawa An-gartcha Wana bulaypulay, guwu-bawana.

Birripa gu-galiya yerrcha aburr-ninya minypa gun-nerranga ngarrinyipa nyibu-nana gun-nerranga rrawa. A-mulpiyana a-ni gun-nerranga gun-nerranga a-wena a-ni wengga, michpa Gu-jingarliya, Gun-nartpa, Gurr-goni, Na-kara rrapa Djinang, Wurlaki a-mulpiyana.

Les a-wena, "jal ngu-nirra marn.gi ngu-ni barra ana-gorrburrwa, ngu-yinmiya barra, wengga rrapa gurrurtu marn.gi ngu-ni barra arr-gorrburrwa."

Figure 5.5. The translation team. Left to right: Shereen Ankin, Ernie Burama, Elva Gindjerakama, Dominic Mason and Betty Ngurrpangurrpa (Margaret Carew).

Michpa Les a-wena "ng-gupa barra wirniny ngunyuna." An-barra yerrcha mirrkmirrka ngunabi-rrana.

Ngatipa nyirri-wena, "Jel gun-gungunyja, wurra an-maliyarra ay-ma barra, ay-barnja barra an-maliyarra wupa wirniny mu-guyinda."

Mun-ngatipa wirniny nyirri-nana barra ana-jekarra, bugula gun-bachirra nyirri-nana mirrka nyirri-jirra nyirri-ninya gochilawa.

Barra ana-jekarra, minypa wirniny mun-nerranga nyirri-gonyjinyjinga.

Mun-gata wirniny mu-gorlkgorlkija. An-gata barra ana-jekarra burr-guya barlmarrk wana.

Mun-geka wirniny ngana mu-jirra wana. Aburr-barrngumarra An-barra yerrcha, lika nyiburr-weya nyiburr-nirra.

Gun-molamola nyiburr-rakija nyiburr-wena nyiburr-ni.

Nipa Les burr-barripuna An-barra yerrcha an-mumurna, wana an-guyinda, bijirri-barripuna Frank Gurrmanamana rrapa Les An-gubarraparra.

Gala aburr-ngekngarna, aburr-benapa lula aburr-ji, marngi aburr-nekarra An-barra wengga, rrapa gurrurtu, gama ny-manga gu-mola nyi-ni barra, gu-molamola jarlakarra ny-bitima barra.

Janguny aburr-weya, ngaypa balaji nguburr-wucha, rrapa gun-guwurlcha bugula nguburr-wucha ngu-nirra.

Ngaypa gama yerrcha nguburr-ganyja mirrka jarriya, rrapa delipa yerrcha, gapala yerrcha.

Mun-gata balaji, diyama, jichicha, mun-banda nyiburr-worlpuna nyiburr-bona.

An-mumurna an-guyinda bulay wenga ana-bamana, nipa an-nelangga Dr Herbert Cole "Nugget" Coombs, 1958 a-bena. Nipa a-wena apala, "Ajay yanma ny-jarlapa skurl."

Ngaypa ngu-jarlapana skurl, Mane djang karirra. Aburr-ngardapa aburr-guyinda gama yerrcha, rrapa wurra yerrcha aburr-bona skurl.

Gu-werranga gu-werranga rrawa, skurl aburr-ji. Gijiya, Na-kara, An-barra, Martay, Gun-nartpa, Wurlaki, Djinang, Gurr-goni, rrapa yi-gaba wenga Miwach, gu-ngardapa a-ninya, school nula.

Ngaypa rrapa Les, nyirri-ninya gun-ngardapa bugula.

Gu-gata wenga ngaypa Les nyirri-jekarra Canberra.

Les gu-borrwurra a-ni janguny gun-molamola.

Nipa Les a-wukurrjinga janguny.

Ngaypa ngu-jekarra wana gu-bapala Canberra jama ngu-ji. Ngaypa ngubin-dimarra delipa yerrcha, Ainslie Public School.

1960 nyirri-jekarra gurda Mane djang karirra.

Les barrwa a-wena burrwa An-barra gu-galiya yerrcha.

Ngatipa nyirri-jekarra gurda, wirniny nyirri-gupuna bukula gu-jirra. Barra ana-jekarra.

Ngu-ninya burrwa, gama yerrcha rrapa delipa yerrcha.

Gipa gun-delipa gu-ji skurl 1958, lika wana gu-ni. Skurl teacher yerrcha marngi burr-nakarra a-ninya, marn.gi burr-nekarra Gu-jingarliya rrapa Kunabidji.

Ngaypa barrwa marn.gi ngu-ni barra balaja.

Ngaypa marngi ngu-ni barra, mun-nerranga mun-nerranga Balaji, minypa ngachu, gulach, wartpirrcha mun-banda, rrapa mun-guji, diyama, gornagochila, an-juwurrgiya, an-nga burr-guta.

Ngaypa marngi ngu-ni barra burlupurr, banaka, bol jibi-yalpa barnda, rrapa jikara, morliya ngu-gamba barra ngu-ni, marn.gi ngu-ninya ngu-bamana.

1958 rrapa 1960, gu-rreparra nyiburr-bona nyibu-nana rrawa gun-guyinda, gapal nyiburr-warrchinga, lika nyiburr-bupiyana majuwa ana-jaranga.

Nipa Les, an-mumurna a-ganyja a-bamana, wurra gun-nika gu-nana a-bona.

Nyuwurr-bona ji-gochila Barlparnarra, nyiburr-gungarlcha rrapa aburr-gungunyja gu-ngardapa nyiburr-bona.

Dr Stuart Scougall rrapa Dorothy Bennett abirriny-bena nyiburr-bona. Marngi abirrinyi-ni abirriny-bona, derrka gubi-ngimarra gun-molamola, Mane djang karirra.

Wigipa nyiburr-bona An-barra yerrcha rrawa aburr-gurrimapa, gu-rreparra nyiburr-bamana.

Ngayburrpa nyiburr-bona Mane djang karirra wenga, Gupanga nyiburr-yunya abirri-jirrapa gun-ngardapa ngorrangurra nyiburr-yu, lika nyiburr-jekarra gurda.

Nuwurra waypa ngatipa nyirri-boyarna, wurra Nancy yokayoka jiny-jaliyana jiny-bambungguna guga, yokayoka jin-nelangga Betty. Nancy jela jinyi-ninya apala. Betty jin-ngarrinyjipa delipa.

Lika nipa wana jinyi-ni, minypa jin-borrmunga jinyi-ni apala. Lika burr-guyi marn.gi nguna-nekarra jinyi-ni, gun-nerranga nguna-gelamajortkurra, an-guwengga gu-guyinda.

Nyiburr-werranga marngi nyiburr-ni nula Rhys Jones, mu-ngoyurra ana-bamana 1972. Nuwurra waypa gun-yagara gu-ni.

Ngatipa nyirri-bena ana-gorrburrwa Gupanga rrapa Lalarr Gu-jirrapa rrapa gun-nerranga gun-nerranga rrawa An-barra gun-goyburrpa. Gu-jingarliya nyiburr-weya.

An-gata gapala gun-nigipa jama gun-nelangga archaeologist.

Nipa marngi a-ni, a-galiyana a-ninya janguny, gun-nerranga gun-nerranga rrawa An-barra gun-nika, gun-guwelamapagapa.

Ngatipa nyirri-yu An-barra gun-nika marn.gi nyirri-ni. Nyirrbu-gurdugurdarrana an-guwelamagapa a-ni a-bona, aburr-yu.

Minypa nyirrbu-gurdagurdarrana, rrawa gubu-ngurrjinga janguny, yakarrarra rrapa joborr gubu-ngurrjinga.

An-anngiya an-maliyarra, an-mama, gun-nyimaga, rrapa gun-nerranga jandarra michpa ngapamarda rrapa lawuk.

An-gaba an-gungarlcha jama aburr-jirra aburr-workiya ANU, nipa wurpa balanda a-jarlapana an-gata an-mama nula a-nacha a-workiya, rrapa an-maliyarra, rrapa gun-nyimaga, rrapa gun-gurrema, nipa wurlpa an-gungarlcha marngi, scientist an-gata murna gu-rrimarra. An-gata Dating Machine an-nelangga.

An-mama a-gutuwurra a-barnjinga Dating Machine, an-gata a-ngurrja barra an-nga gu-yinpa an-guyinda, an-maywa, an-geka.

Rhys a-bena burrwa An-barra yerrcha 1999 gu-ni, gu-mungbuna a-ninya a-bena burrwa. John Chappell bitipa gubirri-mungbuna abirri-ni.

Rhys rrapa John wigipa jama aburr-ji burrwa gu-galiya yerrcha An-barra, Betty Ngurrpangurrpa, Elva Jindjerakama rrapa aburr-werranga.

Aburr-bona aburr-gutuwurra, an-mama, an-maliyarra, gun-nyimaga, jandarra, gu-werranga gu-werranga rrawa gubirri-manga.

An-nga nula abirri-yinagata abirri-nirra, bitipa barra marngi abirri-ni barra, abirri-gungarlcha gun-nga gun-burral, an-guwelamagapa a-ninya.

Gun-guwarr baman, gun-bachirra gu-balawarrchinga burr-guyi, yi-gurrepa rrawa gu-ji gu-bona. Guna-warrchinga bukula gu-jirra gu-yunya.

Bol gu-rrirra rrapa gorragorra gu-warrchinga gu-yurtchinga, gorragorra gu-guyabuna, rrapa bol gu-jupana.

Gun-nerranga bulay giy-bawanapa gun-bachirra, guna-warrchinga, giy-bawana.

Date minypa gun-bachirra rrapa rrawa gun-guwarr, an-guwelamagapa mu-ngoyurra a-ninya, ay-na barra jurra mu-guyinda chapter abirri-jirrapa gun-ngardapa.

Rhys gun-yagara gu-ni, wachpul Canberra, 2001. Gurderda wana gu-rrimarra.

Bugula gun-ngardapa gu-yerrnyjinga, jama abirri-ji, John bitipa.

Betty jiny-bona, a-nana nipa Rhys, wachpul a-yu, lika nuwurra gun-yagara gu-ni.

John Chappell gun-yagara gu-ni rrawa New Zealand, 2018.

Gapa Canberra Sally Brockwell gu-bamagutuwurra jinyi-ni, Rhys gun-nigipa jama. Jama jinyi-ni, an-mama an-maliyarra burr-guta gu-ngardapa gu-nakarra. Ngarrinyjipa jama nyirriny-ji, lika nyirrinyi-lebana butala, jama gun-bitipa.

Aningarra gun-nika rrawa

Dating Machine gu-ngurrjinga arrburrwa gu-galiya yerrcha aburr-yu aburr-workiyana gun-guwarr yorr 300.

Gun-ngardapa a-negiyana an-mama an-maliyarra, a-jurnambuna wupa a-nagiyana an-gata. Gun-nyimaga a-rronga a-workiyana. Burr-guyi a-warrchinga a-ninya waykin. Bulgapulga an-gapala a-negiyana.

Michael Aningarra rrapa aburr-yigipa gapala yerrcha rrapa gu-ngarda yerrcha, abi-rrenyjinga aburr-yu waykin, an-maliyarra, 1972.

An-gata Rhys gu-gata a-barripana an-dirrbula, an-jiwurrgiya, jina-guronggura, rrapa gun-nyimaga, an-guwelamagapa a-barra a-ni.

Gulukula gun-gapula

Gulukula bama a-jirra a-yurra, gun-gapa Gunajangga.

Gulukula a-yurra / Bama an-gorla a-yurra.

Gulukula gun-gapala gu-negarra jorrinyjurra.

Frank Gurrmanamana nyjirri-ganyja nyirri-nana gun-nurda rrawa Gunajangga.

Gun-guna gulukula gun-nigipa rrawa, Gunajangga. Gu-wirrkarra, gu-yerrnyjinga jel, birniny gun-derrartka gu-guyinda, a-gapulawuna, minypa waykin gu-jinyjirra, gun-gapala gu-jarlapuna.

Ngatipa nyirri-barripuna gu-gapala, an-maliyarra an-guyinda, gu-bachirra rrapa jorrinyjurra an-guyinda. Nipa gulukula a-gutuwurra a-barnjinga, gu-ngardapa a-negarra gu-gapalawuna an-maliyarra gun-gapala gu-guyinda.

Dating Machine gu-ngurrjinga arrburrwa gu-galiya yerrcha aburr-yu aburr-workiyana gun-guwarr yorr 900, waygiji gun-guwarr mu-ngoyurra ngayburrpa gala marn.gi.

Guna-jengga rrawa

Guna-jengga yi-gurrepa gochilawa. An-gujechiya mun-dirra abu-gurrmurra jichicha nula.

Rhys rrapa ngaypa nyirri-bona nyirri-workiyana, nyiburr-murra nyiburr-bona. Lika an-murra jichicha a-barrngumurra an-gujechiya gu-guyinda.

Jiny-yarrchinga garriwa jiny-jurnumbuna jin-giya. Nyibu-nana, "ay garriwa jiny-yarrchinga jiny-jarl", nyiburr-yinagata. Lika nyuwu-barripana garriwa jin-giya jin-murra!

An-dirrbula rrapa gun-nyimaga nyirri-barripuna Rhys ngatipa. Balanda yerrcha awu-barnjinga, Dating Machine ana-guyinda, an-maliyarra an-guyinda, an-guwelamagapa awu-barra aburr-ni awurr-workiyana.

Dating Machine gu-ngurrjinga arrburrwa gu-galiya yerrcha aburr-yu aburr-workiyana gun-guwarr yorr 500.

Gupanga wangarr an-dakal a-yurra

Wangarr An-dakal a-yurra, diyama Gupanga a-yunyarra. Nipa Harry Mulumbuk rrapa Barney Girrirrwanga bitipa borrk mbirri-manga, abirri-japurndiyana abirri-ni, diyama. Derrka gubirri-ngimarra, an-gata an-mawunga abirri-barnjinga, an-gartcha rrapa diyama.

Walacha, Ana-wurulja aburr-bapurrurr diyama aburr-japurndiyana aburr-ninya.

Dating Machine gu-ngurrjinga arrburrwa gu-galiya yerrcha aburr-yu aburr-workiyana gun-guwarr yorr 1,450.

Ji-bena rrawa

Ngaypa ngu-borrwuja an-gata Frank nyjirri-ganyja, Rhys rrapa ngaypa. Nyirri-nacha jorrinyjurra nyjirri-ganyja yi-gurrepa Balpilja ji-gochila, waykin gun-gapala Ji-bena.

Frank birripa abi-rrana gornabola lika gardapamba awu-manga, jikara guwu-manga, awu-bachkarrana guga.

Frank a-weya a-nirra, gun-guwarr an-mumurna An-barra a-weya Gu-kuriya rrapa Gun-nartpa aburr-worlpuna, manakarda, bularra ana-mirrka, ganarra an-ganaka an-nga minyjak rrapa balaji. Mu-ngoyurra an-guwelamagapa aburr-yu waykin gu-gapala, gorrogorra gubu-gupuna.

Ngaypa Rhys, nyirri-garrmurra rrapa aburr-werranga An-barra aburr-weya nyiburr-garrmurra nyirrbu-wuna mirrka (handing over), an-maliyarra.

Ngatipa nyirri-barripuna 19 an-nerranga an-nerranga an-maliyarra, burr-gurla an-dirrbula an-burral an-jaranga a-ni.

Rrapa an-mama an-guyinda nyirri-barripuna minypa barnda, gornabola, ngoyumbula, jarrka, jichicha, burdacha. Rrapa lawuk, ngapamarda, bulawak waykin gu-yu gu-gapala.

Dating Machine gu-ngurrjinga arrburrwa gu-galiya yerrcha aburr-yu aburr-workiyana Ji-bena gun-guwarr yorr 1,300.

Jilangga a-jirra

Gu-galiya yerrcha aburr-yu aburr-workiyana Jilangga a-jirra. Airport gubu-jarlapuna awurr-bamana Jimarda, yi-gurrepa. Awurr-wena, "gun-guna yi-gurrepa airport, nyiburr-bupiya barra gochilawa, Yilan."

An-dirrbula an-murra an-gata gu-gapala. Dating Machine gu-ngurrjinga arrburrwa gu-galiya yerrcha aburr-yu aburr-workiyana Jilangga a-jirra gun-guwarr yorr 1,200.

Jinawunya

Gu-galiya yerrcha guwu-mangga gun-menama gubi-yalka, rrapa jingka an-gubay, an-dembarala, ngandipurdudu, an-gujawiya, an-juwurrgiya, diyama, garrmirnimal, rrapa minypa ngukurarrkarrk, gorratola, jumburrich, burlbar, dungunbarra gun-jong gu-guyinda jiny-yurra, rrapa jarrayaba, ngurirra, barnda burr-guta.

Rhys an-garlajawurrga gu-gatiya Jinawunya a-barripuna.

Dating Machine gu-ngurrjinga arrburrwa gu-galiya yerrcha aburr-yu aburr-workiyana Jinawunya gun-guwarr yorr 700.

Jurnaka

Gun-guna Dar A-yurrapa, jurnaka gu-wurrpa.

Rhys ngaypa nyirri-malchinga burrwa gu-galiya yerrcha, minypa rrawa nyuwurr-bona jichicha nyuwu-manga, yuluk rrapa an-gurljuraba bardalal gu-guyinda.

An-dirrbula an-murra an-gata gu-gapala. Dating Machine gu-ngurrjinga arrburrwa gu-galiya yerrcha aburr-yu aburr-workiyana gun-guna rrawa gun-guwarr yorr 400.

Lorrkon a-jirrapa

Lorrkon a-jirrapa, gurda jorrinyjurra. Rhys gu-barripuna lawuk gu-jel gu-yu, Lorrkon a-jirrapa.

Dating Machine gu-ngurrjinga arrburrwa gu-galiya yerrcha aburr-yu aburr-workiyana Lorrkon a-jirrapa gun-guwarr yorr 1,400.

Mu-garnbal

Gun-guna gun-birripa Martay yerrcha.

Barrwa nyiburr-bona lipalipa mu-guyinda, lipalipa mun-nelangga Mu-garnbal. David Bandarrpi, Mary Muna-barlpa, Laurie, Jimmy nyiburr-bona wigipa.

Aburr-gata gu-galiya yerrcha aburr-bona awurr-workiyana gu-gapal, jin-gombula, jarrka aburr-worlpuna. Jin-gombula mu-gorrngunya jiny-yurra jiny-yorkiya, jarrka a-yurra a-workiya gu-rralala gu-guyinda, mbi-ngokurrmurra ana-bena ana-yu, jarrka. Rrapa jina-bena jina-yu, jin-gombula.

Burr-yorrcha (wet season) aburr-yu aburr-workiyana gu-galiya yerrcha gu-gapula, gorragorra gubu-gupuna.

Rhys a-barripuna ana-mula an-ika an-mama gu-gapala. Dating Machine gu-ngurrjinga arrburrwa gu-galiya yerrcha aburr-yu aburr-workiyana Mu-garnbal gun-guwarr yorr 3,700.

Muyu a-jirrapa

Muyu a-jirrapa an-maliyarra gu-gapala a-barripuna.

Barra gun-gata barlmarrk wana a-yerrnyjinga an-maliyarra jorrinyjurra, a-gakija gu-bugula.

Muyu a-jirrapa Rhys an-dirrbula an-maliyarra a-barripuna gu-gapala. Dating Machine gu-ngurrjinga arrburrwa gu-galiya yerrcha aburr-yu aburr-workiyana Muyu a-jirrapa gun-guwarr yorr 1,400.

Ngarli ji-bama

Gu-galiya yerrcha aburr-yu aburr-workiyana mirdawarr.

Ngarli ji-bama Rhys jina-guronggura jin-maliyarra jiny-barripuna. Dating Machine gu-ngurrjinga arrburrwa gu-galiya yerrcha aburr-yu aburr-workiyana Ngarli ji-bama gun-guwarr yorr 300.

Yuluk a-jirrapa

Yuluk a-jirrapa, yi-gurrepa Mardanga a-jirra

Yuluk gu-buna rralala, rrapa gun-gapala, yi-gurrepa Mardanga a-jirra.

Rhys an-dirrbula an-maliyarra rrapa gun-nyimaga a-barripuna gu-gapala. Dating Machine gu-ngurrjinga arrburrwa gu-galiya yerrcha aburr-yu aburr-workiyana Yuluk a-jirrapa gun-guwarr yorr 600.

REFERENCES

Allen, Harry and Pam Rowe (2014). Assessing Donald Thomson's model of seasonal change. *Ethnoarchaeology* 6(1): 61–77.

Bahn, Paul (1992). *Dictionary of Archaeology.* Glasgow: Harper Collins.

Ballard, Chris, Stuart Bedford, Shane Cronin and Sönke Stern (2023). Evidence at source for the mid-fifteenth century eruption of Kuwae, Vanuatu. *Journal of Applied Volcanology* 12: 1–12.

Barham, Anthony, Mike Rowland and G. Hitchcock (2004). Torres Strait *bepotaim*: An overview of archaeological and ethnoarchaeological investigations and research. *Memoirs of the Queensland Museum Cultural Heritage Series* 3(1): 1–72.

Bourke, Patricia (2012). *Late Holocene Indigenous Economies of the Tropical Australian Coast: An Archaeological Study of the Darwin Region.* Oxford: British Archaeological Reports International Series.

Bourke, Patricia (2005). Archaeology of shell mounds of the Darwin coast: Totems of an ancestral landscape. In Patricia Bourke, Sally Brockwell and Clayton Fredericksen, eds. *Darwin Archaeology: Aboriginal, Asian and European Heritage of Australia's Top End*, 29–48. Darwin: CDU Press.

Bourke, Patricia, Sally Brockwell, Patrick Faulkner and Betty Meehan (2007). Climate variability in the mid to late Holocene Arnhem Land region, north Australia: Archaeological archives of environmental and cultural change. In Peter Lape, ed. *Climate Change and Archaeology in the Pacific.* Special edition. *Archaeology in Oceania* 42(3): 91–101.

Brady, Maggie (2013). Drug substances introduced by the Macassans: The mystery of the tobacco pipe. In Marshall Clark and Sally May, eds. *Macassan History and Heritage: Journeys, Encounters and Influences*, 141–58. Canberra: ANU Press.

Brandl, Eric (1988). *Australian Aboriginal Paintings in Western and Central Arnhem Land: Temporal Sequences and Elements of Style in Cadell River and Deaf Adder Creek Art.* Canberra: Australian Institute of Aboriginal Studies.

Brockwell, Sally (2013). "Deadmen and dreamings": Some reflections on *An-barra* archaeology. In Geoff Bailey, Karen Hardy and Abdoulaye Camara, eds. *Shell Energy: Prehistoric Coastal Resource Strategies*, 287–98. Oxford: Oxbow.

Brockwell, Sally (2009). *Archaeological Settlement Patterns and Mobility Strategies on the Lower Adelaide River, Northern Australia.* Oxford: British Archaeological Reports International Series.

Brockwell, Sally (2006). Earth mounds in northern Australia: A review. *Australian Archaeology* 63(1): 47–56.

Brockwell, Sally (2001). Models, mounds and mobility, wetlands archaeology in the Top End: Some comparisons. In Atholl Anderson, Ian Lilley and Sue O'Connor, eds. *Histories of Old Ages: Essays in Honour of Rhys Jones*, 327–42. Canberra: Pandanus Publications, Centre for Archaeological Research, Research School of Pacific and Asian Studies, Australian National University.

Brockwell, Sally, Patricia Bourke, Anne Clarke, Christine Crassweller, Patrick Faulkner, Betty Meehan et al. (2011). Holocene settlement of the northern coastal plains, Northern Territory. *The Beagle Records of the Museums and Art Galleries of the Northern Territory* 27: 1–22.

Brockwell, Sally, Patrick Faulkner, Patricia Bourke, Anne Clarke, Christine Crassweller, Daryl Guse et al. (2009). Radiocarbon dates from the Top End: A cultural chronology for the Northern Territory coastal plains. *Australian Aboriginal Studies* 1: 54–76.

Brockwell, Sally, Ben Marwick, Patricia Bourke, Patrick Faulkner and Richard Willan (2013). Late Holocene climate change and human behavioural variability in the coastal wet-dry tropics of northern Australia: Evidence from a pilot study of oxygen isotopes in marine bivalve shells from archaeological sites. *Australian Archaeology* 76: 21–33.

Brockwell, Sally, Betty Meehan and Betty Ngurrabangurraba (2005). The *An-barra* Archaeological Project: A progress report. *Australian Aboriginal Studies* 1: 84–9.

Brockwell, Sally, Colin Pardoe, Mirani Litster, Daryl Wesley, Jillian Huntley, Morgan Disspain et al. (2020). Human responses to the late Holocene freshwater transition on the northern coastal plains of the Alligator Rivers region in western Arnhem Land. *Australian Archaeology* 86(1): 80–94.

Bronk Ramsey, Christopher (2024). OxCal v4.4.4 [Web interface build number: 173] program for radiocarbon calibration. Accessed 14 March 2025: https://c14.arch.ox.ac.uk/oxcal.html.

Bronk Ramsey, Christopher (2009). Bayesian analysis of radiocarbon dates. *Radiocarbon* 51: 337–60.

Bureau of Meteorology (BOM) (2024). Summary statistics for Maningrida. Climate statistics for Australian locations. BOM website. Accessed 14 March 2025: Australia's official weather forecasts & weather radar – Bureau of Meteorology (bom.gov.au).

Carmichael, Bethune (2015). *Places in Peril: Archaeology in the Anthropocene.* Vimeo. Accessed 14 March 2025: https://vimeo.com/203773921.

Chaloupka, George (1993). *Journey in Time: The World's Longest Continuing Art Tradition: The 50,000 Year Story of the Australian Aboriginal Rock Art of Arnhem Land.* Sydney: Reed.

Chappell, John (2001). Geomorphology and Holocene geology of coastal and estuarine plains of northern Australia. *Geological Society of Australia Special Publication* 21: 303–14.

Chappell, John (1988). Geomorphological dynamics and evolution of tidal river and floodplain systems in northern Australia. In Deborah Wade-Marshall and Peter Loveday, eds. *Floodplains Research*, vol. 2, *Northern Australia: Progress and Prospects*, 34–57. Darwin: North Australia Research Unit, Australian National University.

Chappell, John and Rhys Jones (1999). Holocene environmental and cultural changes in northern Arnhem Land. *RSES Annual Report.* Canberra: Research School of Earth Sciences, Australian National University.

Chappell, John and Colin Woodroffe (1985). Morphodynamics of Northern Territory tidal rivers and floodplains. In Kristin Bardsley, Jim Davie and Colin Woodroffe, eds. *Coasts and Tidal Wetlands of the Australian Monsoon Region*, 85–96. Mangrove Monograph 1. Darwin: North Australia Research Unit, Australian National University.

Christian, Clifford and George Stewart (1953). *General Report on the Survey of the Katherine-Darwin Region*, 1946. Land Research Series No.1. Canberra: Commonwealth Scientific and Industrial Research Organisation (CSIRO).

Claassen, Cheryl (1998). *Shells.* Cambridge: Cambridge University Press.

Clark, Marshall and Sally May, eds. (2013). *Macassan History and Heritage: Journeys, Encounters and Influences.* Canberra: ANU Press.

Clark, Robin and Joan Guppy (1988). A transition from mangrove forest to freshwater wetland in the monsoon tropics of Australia. *Journal of Biogeography* 15: 665–84.

Clarke, Anne (2002). The ideal and the real: Cultural and personal transformations of archaeological research on Groote Eylandt, northern Australia. *World Archaeology* 34(2): 249–64.

Clarke, Anne and Ursula Frederick (2006). Closing the distance: Interpreting cross-cultural engagements through Indigenous rock art. In Ian Lilley, ed. *Archaeology of Oceania: Australia and the Pacific Islands*, 116–33. Malden: Blackwell.

Clarkson, Chris, Zenobia Jacobs, Ben Marwick, Richard Fullagar, Lynley Wallis, Mike Smith et al. (2017). Human occupation of Australia by 65,000 years. *Nature* 547 (7663): 306–10.

Clune, Genevieve and Rodney Harrison (2009). Coastal shell middens of the Abydos coastal plain, Western Australia. *Archaeology in Oceania* 44 (Supplement): 70–80.

Clunies Ross, Margaret and Stephen Wild (1982). *Djambidj: An Aboriginal Song Series from Northern Australia.* A companion book for the stereo recording on LP disc and cassette of the performance by Frank Gurrmanamana and Frank Malkorda (singers) and Sam Gumugun (*didjerridu*) at the Goethe Institute, Canberra, May 1979. Canberra: Australian Institute of Aboriginal Studies.

Cochrane, Grant (2014). *Marcia hiantina* shell matrix sites at Norman Creek, western Cape York Peninsula. *Australian Archaeology* 78(1): 47–52.

Cribb, Roger (1996). Shell mounds, domiculture and ecosystem manipulation on western Cape York Peninsula. In P. Veth and P. Hiscock, eds. *Archaeology of Northern Australia*, 150–73. Tempus 4. St Lucia: Anthropology Museum, University of Queensland.

Culture, History and Language (CHL) (2024). On the Kuwae trail. Canberra: College of Asia and the Pacific, Australian National University. Accessed 13 March 2025: https://chl.anu.edu.au/content-centre/article/series/kuwae-trail.

David, Bruno and Mura Badulgal (2006). What happened in Torres Strait 400 years ago? Ritual transformations in an island seascape. *Journal of Island and Coastal Archaeology* 1(2): 123–43.

David, Bruno, Joanna FreslØv, Russell Mullett, GunaiKurnai Land and Waters Aboriginal Corporation, Jean-Jacques Delannoy, Matthew McDowell et al. (2021). 50 years and worlds apart: Rethinking the Holocene occupation of Cloggs Cave (East Gippsand, SE Australia) five decades after its initial excavation and in light of GunaiKurnai world views. *Australian Archaeology* 87(1): 1–20.

David, Bruno, Russell Mullett, Nathan Wright, Birgitta Stephenson, Jeremy Ash, Joanna FreslØv et al. (2024). Archaeological evidence of an ethnographically documented Australian Aboriginal ritual dated to the last Ice Age. *Nature Human Behaviour* 8: 1481–92.

David, Bruno, Paul Taçon, Jean-Jacques Delannoy and Jean-Michel Geneste (2017). *The Archaeology of Rock Art in Western Arnhem Land, Australia.* Terra Australis 47. Canberra: ANU Press.

David, Bruno and Marshall Weisler (2006). Kurturnia Iwa K (Ba Du) and the archaeology of villages in Torres Strait. *Australian Archaeology.* Accessed 6 April 2025: https://www.academia.edu/898291/Kurturniaiwak_Badu_and_the_archaeology_of_villages_in_Torres_Strait.

David, Bruno and Meredith Wilson (1999). Re-reading the landscape: Place and identity in NE Australia during the late Holocene. *Cambridge Archaeological Journal* 9(2): 163–88.

Faulkner, Patrick (2013). *Life on the Margins: An Archaeological Investigation of Late Holocene Economic Variability, Coastal Blue Mud Bay, Northern Australia.* Canberra. ANU Press.

Faulkner, Patrick, Jennifer Miller, Erendira Quintana Morales, Alison Crowther, Ceri Shipton, Emmanuel Ndiema et al. (2021). 67,000 years of coastal engagement at Panga ya Saidi, eastern Africa. *PLoS ONE* 16: 1–29. https://doi.org/10.1371/journal.pone.0256761.

Frederick, Ursula and Anne Clarke (2011). Making a sea change: Rock art, archaeology and the enduring legacy of Frederick McCarthy's research on Groote Eylandt. In Martin Thomas and Margot Neale, eds. *Exploring the Legacy of the 1948 Arnhem Land Expedition*, 135–55. Canberra: ANU Press.

Fullagar, Richard, Betty Meehan and Rhys Jones (1999). Residue analysis of ethnographic plant-working and other tools from northern Australia. In Patricia Anderson, ed. *Prehistory of Agriculture: New Experimental and Ethnographic Approaches*, 15–25. Monograph 40. Los Angeles: Institute of Archaeology, University of California.

Gillett, Ross (1981). The Northern Patrol. *Naval Historical Review.* Accessed 14 March 2025: https://navyhistory.au/the-northern-patrol/.

Glasgow, Kathleen (1994). *Burarra Gun-artpa Dictionary with English Finder List: Based on the Language Shared by Speakers of the An-barra, Martay and Gun-artpa Dialects.* Darwin: Summer Institute of Linguistics.

Goodfellow, Denise (1993). *Fauna of Kakadu and the Top End.* Kent Town: Wakefield Press.

Grant, Arch (1995). *Aliens in Arnhem Land.* Dee Why: Frontier Publishing.

Guilfoyle, David, Myles Mitchell, Cat Morgan, Harley Coyne and Vernice Gillies (2013). Exploring the role of archaeology within Indigenous natural resource management: A case study from Western Australia. In Sally Brockwell, Sue O'Connor and Denis Byrne, eds. *Transcending the Culture–Nature Divide in*

Cultural Heritage: Views from the Asia-Pacific Region, 101–16. Terra Australis 36. Canberra: ANU Press.

Gurrmanamana, Frank, Les Hiatt and Kim McKenzie (2002). *People of the Rivermouth: The Joborr Texts of Frank Gurrmanamana.* Canberra: National Museum of Australia and Aboriginal Studies Press.

Hamilton, Annette (1981). *Nature and Nurture: Aboriginal Child-Rearing in North-Central Arnhem Land.* Canberra: Australian Institute of Aboriginal Studies.

Hanks, Peter and Bryan Keon-Cohen, eds. (1984). *Aborigines and the Law: Essays in the Memory of Elizabeth Eggleston.* Sydney: George Allen & Unwin.

Harris, Matthew, Marshall Weisler and Patrick Faulkner (2015). A refined protocol for calculating MNI in archaeological molluscan shell assemblages: A Marshall Islands case study. *Journal of Archaeological Science* 57: 168–79.

Harrison, Rodney (2009). The archaeology of the Port Hedland coastal plain and implications for understanding the prehistory of shell mounds and middens in northwestern Australia. *Archaeology in Oceania* 44 (Supplement): 81–98.

Haultain, Charles (1971). *Watch off Arnhem Land.* Canberra: Roebuck Society.

Heaton, Timothy, Peter Köhler, Martin Butzin, Edouard Bard, Ron Reimer, William Austin et al. (2020). Marine20—The marine radiocarbon age calibration curve (0–55,000 cal BP). *Radiocarbon* 62(4): 779–820.

Hiatt, Lester (1965). *Kinship and Conflict: A Study of an Aboriginal Community in Northern Arnhem Land.* Canberra: Australian National University.

Hiscock, Peter (2013). Beyond the Dreamtime: Archaeology and explorations of religious change in Australia. *World Archaeology* 45(1): 124–36.

Hiscock, Peter (2008). *Archaeology of Ancient Australia.* London: Routledge.

Hiscock, Peter (1997). Archaeological evidence for environmental change in Darwin Harbour. In J.R. Hanley, G. Caswell, Dirk Megirian and Helen Larson, eds. *The Marine Flora and Fauna of Darwin Harbour, Northern Territory, Australia: Proceedings of the Sixth International Marine Biological Workshop*, 445–9. Darwin and Perth: Museum and Art Gallery of the Northern Territory and Western Australian Museum.

Hiscock, Peter and Patrick Faulkner (2006). Dating the Dreaming? Creation of myths and rituals for mounds along the northern Australian coastline. *Cambridge Archaeological Journal* 16(2): 209–22.

Hogg, Alan, Timothy Heaton, Quan Hua, J. Palmer, Chris Turney, Jonathan Southon et al. (2020). SHCal20 Southern Hemisphere calibration, 0–55,000 years cal BP. *Radiocarbon* 62(4): 759–78.

Holdaway, Simon and Harry Allen (2011). A retrospective review of Richard A. Gould's Living Archaeology. *Ethnoarchaeology* 3(2): 203–20.

Holdaway, Simon, Patricia Fanning, Fiona Petchey, Kasey Allely, Justin Shiner and Geoffrey Bailey (2017). Temporal variability in shell mound formation at Albatross Bay, northern Australia. *PLoS ONE* 12(8): e0183863. https://doi.org/10.1371/journal. Pone.0183863.

Hope, Geoff, Philip Hughes and Jeremy Russell-Smith (1985). Geomorphological fieldwork and the evolution of the landscape of Kakadu National Park. In Rhys Jones, ed. *Archaeological Research in Kakadu National Park*, 229–40. Special Publication 13. Canberra: Australian National Parks and Wildlife Service.

Jones, Rhys, ed. (1985a). *Archaeological Research in Kakadu National Park*. Special Publication 13. Canberra: Australian National Parks and Wildlife Service.

Jones, Rhys (1985b). Ordering the landscape. In Ian Donaldson and Tamsin Donaldson, eds. *Seeing the First Australians*, 181–209. Sydney: George Allen & Unwin.

Jones, Rhys (1980). Hunters in the Australian coastal savanna. In David Harris, ed. *Human Ecology in Savanna Environments*, 107–46. London: Academic Press.

Jones, Rhys and Jim Bowler (1980). Struggle for the savanna: Northern Australia in ecological and prehistoric perspective. In Rhys Jones, ed. *Northern Australia: Options and Implications*, 3–31. Canberra: Research School of Pacific Studies, Australian National University.

Jones, Rhys and Ian Johnson (1985). Deaf Adder Gorge: Lindner site, Nauwalabila 1. In Rhys Jones, ed. *Archaeological Research in Kakadu National Park*, 183–227. Special Publication 13. Canberra: Australian National Parks and Wildlife Service.

Jones, Rhys and Betty Meehan (1989). Past and present foods of the *Gidjingali*: Ethnographic and archaeological perspectives from northern Australia on tuber and seed exploitation. In David Harris and Gordon Hillman, eds. *Foraging and Farming: The Evolution of Plant Exploitation*, 120–35. London: Unwin Hyman.

Kamminga, Johan and Harry Allen (1973). *Report of the Archaeological Survey*. Alligator Rivers Environmental Fact-Finding Study. Darwin: Government Printer.

MacFarlane, Ingereth, Mary-Jane Mountain and Robert Payton, eds. (2005). *Many Exchanges: Archaeology, History, Community and the Work of Isabel McBryde*. Aboriginal History Monograph 11. Canberra: ANU Press.

MacKnight, Campbell (1976). *The Voyage to Marege: Macassan Trepangers in Northern Australia*. Melbourne: Melbourne University Press.

May, Sally, Paul Taçon, Daryl Wesley and Meg Travers (2010). Painting history: Indigenous observations and depictions of the "other" in NW Arnhem Land. *Australian Archaeology* 71: 57–65.

May, Sally, Paul Taçon, Duncan Wright and Melissa Marshall (2015). The rock art of Kakadu: Past, present and future research, conservation and management. In

Steve Winderlich, ed. *Walk the Talk: Cultural Heritage Management in Kakadu National Park*, 36–44. Kakadu National Park Symposium 6. Darwin: Australian Government.

McCarthy, Frederick and Frank Setzler (1960). The archaeology of Arnhem Land. In Charles Mountford, ed. *Records of the American-Australian Scientific Expedition to Arnhem Land*, vol. 2, *Anthropology and Nutrition*, 215–95. Melbourne: Melbourne University Press.

McDonald, N. and John McAlpine (1991). Floods and droughts: The northern climate. In Christopher Haynes, Michael Ridpath and Martin Williams, eds. *Monsoonal Australia: Landscape, Ecology and Man in the Northern Lowlands*, 19–29. Rotterdam: A.A. Balkema.

McGowan, Hamish, Samuel Marx, Patrick Moss and Andrew Hammond (2012). Evidence of ENSO mega-drought triggered collapse of prehistory Aboriginal society in northwest Australia. *Geophysical Research Letters* 39(22): L22702.

McKenzie, Kim (1980). *Waiting for Harry*. Documentary. Canberra: Australian Institute of Aboriginal Studies.

McNiven, Ian (2016). The ethnographic echo: Archaeological approaches to writing long-term histories of Indigenous spiritual beliefs and ritual practices. *The Journal of the Australian Academy of the Humanities* 7: 8–21.

McNiven, Ian (2006). Dauan 4 and the emergence of ethnographically-known social arrangements across Torres Strait during the last 600–800 years. *Australian Archaeology* 62: 1–12.

Meehan, Betty (1995). The *Anbarra* Archaeological Project 1970 – present. In Iain Davidson, Christine Lovell-Jones and Robyne Bancroft, eds. *Archaeologists and Aborigines Working Together*, 38–40. Armidale: University of New England.

Meehan, Betty (1991). Wetland hunters: Some reflections. In Christopher Haynes, Michael Ridpath and Martin Williams, eds. *A Northern Heritage: Landscape, Ecology and Man in Monsoonal Lowlands in Australia*, 197–206. Rotterdam: A.A. Balkema.

Meehan, Betty (1988a). Changes in Aboriginal exploitation of wetlands in northern Australia. In Deborah Wade-Marshall and Peter Loveday, eds. *Northern Australia: Progress and Prospects*, vol. 2, Appendix 2, 1–23. Darwin: North Australia Research Unit, Australian National University.

Meehan, Betty (1988b). The "dinner time camp": Its uses and abuses in archaeological interpretation. In Betty Meehan and Rhys Jones, eds. *Archaeology with Ethnography: An Australian Perspective*, 171–81. Proceedings of the 1983 Australian Archaeological Association Conference in Canberra. Canberra:

Department of Prehistory, Research School of Pacific Studies, Australian National University.

Meehan, Betty (1983). A matter of choice? Some thoughts on shell gathering strategies in northern Australia. In Caroline Grigson and Juliet Clutton-Brock, eds. *Animals and Archaeology: Shell Middens, Fishes and Birds*, 3–17. Oxford: British Archaeological Reports.

Meehan, Betty (1982a). *Shell Bed to Shell Midden.* Canberra: Australian Institute of Aboriginal Studies.

Meehan, Betty (1982b). "Ten fish for one man": Some *Anbarra* attitudes towards food and health. In Janice Reid, ed. *Body, Land and Spirit: Health and Healing in Aboriginal Society*, 96–120. St Lucia: Queensland University Press.

Meehan, Betty and Rhys Jones (2005). Stone tool use in land with no stone: Ethnographic notes from the *Gu-jinarliya.* In Ian MacFarlane, Mary-Jane Mountain and Robert Payton, eds. *Many Exchanges: Archaeology, History, Community and the Work of Isabel McBryde*, 147–69. Aboriginal History Monograph 11. Canberra: ANU Press.

Meehan, Betty and Rhys Jones, eds (1988). *Archaeology with Ethnography: An Australian Perspective.* Proceedings of the 1983 Australian Archaeological Association Conference in Canberra. Canberra: Department of Prehistory, Research School of Pacific Studies, Australian National University.

Meehan, Betty and Rhys Jones (1986). Hunter-gatherer diet: An archaeological perspective and ethnographic method. In T. Geoffrey Taylor and N.K. Jenkins, eds. *Proceedings of the XIII International Congress of Nutrition*, 951–5. London: John Libbey.

Meehan, Betty and Rhys Jones (1980). The outstation movement and hints of a white backlash. In Rhys Jones, ed. *Northern Australia: Options and Implications*, 131–57. Canberra: Research School of Pacific Studies, Australian National University.

Meehan, Betty, Rhys Jones and Annie Vincent (1999). *Gula-kula*: Dogs in Anbarra Society, Arnhem Land. In Luise Hercus and Grace Koch, eds. *Sally White Commemorative Edition. Aboriginal History* 23: 83–106. Canberra: School of Humanities, Australian National University

Meehan, Betty, Prue Gaffey and Rhys Jones (1979). Fire to steel: Aboriginal exploitation of *Pandanus* and some wider implications. *Occasional Papers in Anthropology* 9: 73–96. St Lucia: Anthropology Museum, University of Queensland.

Merlan, Francesca, John Morton and Alan Rumsey, eds. (1997). *Scholar and Sceptic: Australian Aboriginal Studies in Honour of L.R. Hiatt.* Canberra: Aboriginal Studies Press.

Mitchell, Scott (1996). Dugongs and dugouts, sharptacks and shellbacks: Macassan contact and Aboriginal marine hunting on the Coburg Peninsula, north western Arnhem Land. *Bulletin of the Indo-Pacific Prehistory Association* 15: 181–91.

Molle, Guillaume, Jean-Marie Wadrawane, Louis Lagarde and Duncan Wright (2023). The sacred stone from the sea: Archaeological and ethnographic perspectives on the ritual value of coral across the Pacific. *Archaeology in Oceania* 58(1): 40–55.

Morrison, Michael (2015). Late Holocene Aboriginal shellfish production strategies in northern Australia: Insights from Prunung (Red Beach), Weipa, Cape York Peninsula. *Queensland Archaeological* Research 18: 1–27.

Morrison, Michael (2014). Chronological trends in late Holocene shell mound construction across northern Australia: Insights from Albatross Bay, Cape York Peninsula. *Archaeology in Oceania* 79(1): 1–13.

Morrison, Michael (2013). From scatter to mound: A new developmental model for shell mound sites at Weipa. *Queensland Archaeological Research* 16: 165–84.

Morrison, Michael (2003). Old boundaries and new horizons: The Weipa shell mounds reconsidered. *Archaeology in Oceania* 38(1): 1–8.

Morphy, Frances, Howard Morphy, Patrick Faulkner and Marcus Barber (2020). Toponyms from 3000 years ago? Implications for the history and structure of the *Yolŋu* social formation in north-east Arnhem Land. *Archaeology in Oceania* 55(3): 153–67.

Mulrennan, Monica and Colin Woodroffe (1998). Holocene development of the lower Mary River plains, Northern Territory, Australia. *The Holocene* 8(5): 565–79.

Mulvaney, Derek John (1975). *The Prehistory of Australia.* Harmondsworth: Penguin.

Northern Standard (1938). Seizure of Japanese luggers: Appeal case in the Supreme Court. 21 June, 10. Trove website accessed 14 March 2025: https://trove.nla.gov.au/newspaper/article/49448669/3236386.

O'Connor, Sue (1999). A diversity of coastal economies: Shell mounds in the Kimberley region in the Holocene. In Jay Hall and Ian McNiven, eds. *Australian Coastal Archaeology*. Research Papers in Archaeology and Natural History, no. 31, 37–50. Canberra: Australian National University.

O'Connor, Sue and Marjorie Sullivan (1994). Distinguishing middens and cheniers: A case study from the southern Kimberley, Western Australia. *Archaeology in Oceania* 29(1): 16–28.

Oertle, Annette, Matthew Leavesley, Sean Ulm, Geraldine Mate and Daniel Rosendahl (2014). At the margins: archaeological evidence for Macassan activities in the South Wellesley Islands, Gulf of Carpentaria. *Australasian Historical Archaeology* 32: 64-71.

Ó Foghlú, Billy (2017). Sustaining cultural identity through environmental sustainability: Earth mounds in northern Australia, c. 2,200 BP to present. In Julien Favreau and Robert Patalano, eds. *Shallow Pasts, Endless Horizons: Sustainability and Archaeology. Proceedings of the 48th Annual Chacmool Conference*, 51–73. Calgary: Chacmool Archaeological Association, University of Calgary.

Oliver, Pamela (2006). *Empty North: Japanese Presence and Australian Reactions 1860s to 1942*. Darwin: CDU Press.

Ortiz-Burgos, Selene (2016). Shannon-Weaver Diversity Index. In Michael J. Kennished. *Encyclopedia of Estuaries*. Encyclopedia of Earth Sciences Series. Dordrecht: Springer. https://doi.org/10.1007/978-94-017-8801-4_233.

Peterson, Nicolas (2003). *Donald Thomson in Arnhem Land*. Melbourne: Melbourne University Press.

Peterson, Nicolas (1973). Campsite locations amongst Australian hunter-gatherers. *Archaeology and Physical Anthropology in Oceania* 8: 173–93.

Reeves, Jessica, Timothy Barrows, Timothy Cohen, Anthony Kiem, Helen Bostock, Kathryn Fitzsimmons et al. (2013). Climate variability over the last 35,000 years recorded in marine and terrestrial archives in the Australian region: An OZ-INTIMATE compilation. *Quaternary Science Reviews* 74: 21–34.

Roberts, Andrew (1994). Cultural landmarks: The Milingimbi mounds. In Marjorie Sullivan, Sally Brockwell and Anne Webb, eds. *Archaeology in the North: Proceedings of the 1993 Australian Archaeological Association Conference*, 176–87. Darwin: North Australia Research Unit, Australian National University.

Ross, Anne, Sean Ulm and Brian Tobane (2013). *Gummingurru*: A community knowledge journey. *Australian Archaeology* 76(1): 62–68.

Rowe, Cassandra, Michael Brand, Lindsay Hutley, Christopher Wurster, Costijn Zwart, Vlad Levchenko et al. (2019). Holocene savanna dynamics in the seasonal tropics of northern Australia. *Review of Palaeobotany and Palynology* 267: 17–31.

Schrire, C. (1982). *The Alligator Rivers: Prehistory and Ecology in Western Arnhem Land*. Terra Australis 7. Canberra: Department of Prehistory, Research School of Pacific Studies, Australian National University.

Shine, Denis, Duncan Wright, Tim Denham, Ken Aplin, Peter Hiscock, Kim Parker et al. (2013). Birriwilk rock shelter: A mid- to late Holocene site in Manilikarr Country, southwest Arnhem Land, Northern Territory. *Australian Archaeology* 76(1): 69–78.

Shiner, Justin, Patricia Fanning, Simon Holdaway, Fiona Petchey, Kasey Beresford, Eloise Hoffman et al. (2013). Shell mounds as the basis for understanding human-environment interaction in far north Queensland, Australia. *Queensland Archeological Research* 66: 65–91.

Sim, Robin and Lynley Wallis (2008). Northern Australian offshore island use during the Holocene. *Australian Archaeology* 67: 95–106.

Stevenson, Janelle, Sally Brockwell, Cassandra Rowe, Ulrike Proske and Justin Shiner (2015). The palaeo-environmental history of Big Willum Swamp, Weipa: An environmental context for the archaeological record. *Australian Archaeology* 80(1): 17–31.

Sweeney, Gordon (1939). Report of Survey in the Liverpool-Blyth River Region, July-August 1939. Unpublished report. Darwin: Northern Territory Administration.

Swete Kelly, Mary Clare and Sarah Phear (2004). Weston Store: Report on the Salvage of Materials from the Weston Storage Facility. Unpublished report. Canberra: Department of Archaeology and Natural History, Australian National University.

Taçon, Paul and Sally Brockwell (1995). Arnhem Land prehistory in landscape, stone and paint. *Transitions: Pleistocene to Holocene in Australia and Papua New Guinea. Antiquity*. Special Edition 69(264): 676–95.

Thomas, Jadeyn, Annie Ross, Shannon Bauwens and Conrad Bauwens (2023). Resurrecting the power in the stones: Developing a modern narrative of the agency and sentience of powerful stones and recreating shared knowledge encounters at *Gummingurru* and its associated site architecture. *Archaeology in Oceania* 58(2): 5–19.

Thurtell, Lisa, C. Max Finalyson, Dean Yibarbuk and Michael Storrs (1999). *The Blyth-Liverpool Wetlands, Arnhem Land, Northern Australia: Information for Management Planning*. Jabiru: Institute of the Supervising Scientist, Environment Australia.

Ulm, Sean, Damien O'Grady, Fiona Petchey, Quan Hua, Geraldine Jacobsen, Lauren Linnenlucke et al. (2023). Australian marine radiocarbon reservoir effects: ΔR atlas and ΔR calculator for Australian mainland coasts and near-shore islands. *Radiocarbon* 65(5): 1139–59.

Urwin, Chris, Lynette Russell and Robert John Skelly (2024). Building culturally meaningful chronologies: Negotiating Indigenous and Western temporalities in Oceania. *Archaeology in Oceania* 59(3): 465–78.

Urwin, Chris, John Bradley, Ian McNiven, Lynette Russell and Lily Yulianti Farid (2023). Re-assessing regional chronologies for island southeast Asian voyaging to Aboriginal Australia. *Archaeology in Oceania* 58: 245–74.

Veitch, Bruce (1999). Shell middens on the Mitchell Plateau: A reflection of a wider phenomenon? In Jay Hall and Ian McNiven, eds. *Australian Coastal Archaeology*. Research Papers in Archaeology and Natural History, no. 31, 51–64. Canberra: Australian National University.

Wesley, Daryl, Mirani Litster and Sue O'Connor (2018). The archaeology of Maliwawa: 25,000 years of occupation in the Wellington Range, Arnhem Land. *Australian Archaeology* 84(2): 108–28.

Wesley, Daryl, Sue O'Connor and Jack Fenner (2016). Re-evaluating the timing of the Indonesian trepang industry in north-west Arnhem Land: Chronological investigations at Malara (Anuru Bay A). *Archaeology in Oceania* 51(3): 169–95.

White, Neville, Betty Meehan, Les Hiatt and Rhys Jones (1990). Demography of contemporary hunter-gatherers: Lessons from Arnhem Land. In Betty Meehan and Neville White, eds. *Hunter-Gatherer Demography: Past and Present*, Oceania Monograph 39, 171–85. Sydney: University of Sydney.

White, Neville and Peter Parsons (1976). Population genetic, social, linguistic and topographical relationships in north-eastern Arnhem Land, Australia. *Nature* 261(5557): 223–5.

White, Neville and Peter Parsons (1973). Genetic and socio-cultural differentiation in the Aborigines of Arnhem Land, Australia. *American Journal of Physical Anthropology* 38(1): 5–14.

Wild, Stephen, ed. (1986). *Rom: An Aboriginal Ritual of Diplomacy*. Canberra: Australian Institute of Aboriginal Studies.

Wild, Stephen (1983). *Rom* in Canberra. *Australian Aboriginal Studies* 1: 55–9.

Williams, Alan, Sean Ulm, Tom Sapienza, Stephen Lewis and Chris Turney (2018). Sea-level change and demography during the last glacial termination and early Holocene across the Australian continent. *Quaternary Science Reviews* 182: 144–54.

Williams, Alan, Sean Ulm, Chris Turney, David Rodhe and Gentry White (2015). The establishment of complex society in prehistoric Australia: Demographic and mobility changes in the late Holocene. *PloS ONE* 10(6): e0128661.

Woodroffe, Colin (1988). Changing mangrove and wetland habitats over the last 8000 years: Northern Australia and Southeast Asia. In Deborah Wade-Marshall and Peter Loveday, eds. *Floodplains Research*, vol. 2, *Northern Australia: Progress and Prospects*, 1–23. Darwin: North Australia Research Unit, Australian National University.

Woodroffe, Colin, Bruce Thom and John Chappell (1985). Development of widespread mangrove swamps in mid-Holocene times. *Nature* 317: 711–13.

Wright, Duncan, Ladislav Nejman, Steve Skitmore, Wayne Brennan, Rebecca Parkes, Ronald Lamilami et al. (2023). Archaeology of animate ancestors and entanglement at *Mayarnjarn* in the Wellington Range region, Northern Territory. *Archaeology in Oceania* 58(2): 172–82.

Wright, Duncan, Cygnet Repu and Falen Passi (2021). The "Waiat Archeology Project" in Torres Strait, northern Australia. *Antiquity* 95(379): e5, 1–9.

Xu, Guanmian (2021). Pepper to Sea Cucumbers: Chinese Gustatory Revolution in Global History, 900–1840. Unpublished PhD thesis, Leiden: Leiden University.

Appendix 1
AN-BARRA BIBLIOGRAPHY

Brockwell, Sally (2013). "Deadmen and dreamings": Some reflections on *An-barra* archaeology. In Geoff Bailey, Karen Hardy and Abdoulaye Camara, eds. *Shell Energy: Prehistoric Coastal Resource Strategies*, 287–98. Oxford: Oxbow.

Brockwell, Sally, Betty Meehan and Betty Ngurrabangurraba (2005). The *Anbarra* archaeological project: A progress report. *Australian Aboriginal Studies* 1: 84–9.

Fullagar, Richard, Betty Meehan and Rhys Jones (1999). Residue analysis of ethnographic plant-working and other tools from northern Australia. In Patricia Anderson, ed. *Prehistory of Agriculture: New Experimental and Ethnographic Approaches*, 15–25. Monograph 40. Los Angeles: Institute of Archaeology, University of California.

Glasgow, Kathleen (1994). *Burarra Gun-artpa Dictionary with English Finder List: Based on the Language Shared by Speakers of the An-barra, Martay and Gun-artpa Dialects.* Darwin: Summer Institute of Linguistics.

Gurrmanamana, Frank, Les Hiatt and Kim McKenzie (2002). *People of the Rivermouth: The Joborr Texts of Frank Gurrmanamana.* Canberra: National Museum of Australia and Aboriginal Studies Press.

Hamilton, Annette (1981). *Nature and Nurture: Aboriginal Child-Rearing in North-Central Arnhem Land.* Canberra: Australian Institute of Aboriginal Studies.

Hiatt, Lester (1965). *Kinship and Conflict: A Study of an Aboriginal Community in Northern Arnhem Land.* Canberra: Australian National University.

Jones, Rhys (2000). *Gun-gugaliya Rrawa*, place, ochre and death: A perspective from Aboriginal Australia. In Stephen Aldhouse-Green, ed. *Paviland Cave and the "Red Lady": A Definitive Report*, 247–64. Bristol: Western Academic and Specialist Press.

Jones, Rhys (1990). Hunters of the Dreaming: Some ideational, economic and ecological parameters of the Australian Aboriginal productive system. In Doug Yen and Janine Mummery, eds. *Pacific Production Systems: Approaches to Economic*

Prehistory, 25–53. Occasional Papers in Prehistory, No.18. Canberra: Department of Prehistory, Research School of Pacific Studies, Australian National University.

Jones, Rhys (1984). Prehistory in the Australian tropics. In Brian Hughes and John Eedle, eds. *Northern Studies: Report of a Workshop*, 73–91. Darwin: Northern Territory University Planning Authority.

Jones, Rhys (1983). Arnhemland: Life on the edge of the water. In Robert Brissenden, Rosemary Brissenden and Jutta Hosel, eds. *Gift of the Forest*, 102–5. Sydney: Australian Conservation Foundation.

Jones, Rhys (1981). Hunters of Arnhemland: A perspective from the Pleistocene to the present. Union International de Ciencias Prehistoricas y Protohistoricas.. (Miembro del Consejo International de Filosofia y de las Ciencias Humanas de la Unesco, Paris), X Congreso, Mexico, October 19–24. *Resumenes de Comunicaciones, Seccion 1V, Paleolitico Superior*, 90–1.

Jones, Rhys (1980a). Cleaning the country: The *Gindjingali* and their Arnhemland environment. *BHP Journal* 1: 10–15.

Jones, Rhys (1980b). Hunters in the Australian coastal savanna. In David Harris, ed. *Human Ecology in Savanna Environments*, 107–46. London: Academic Press.

Jones, Rhys (1975). The Neolithic Palaeolithic and the hunting gardeners: Man and land in the antipodes. In R. Patrick Suggate and M.M. Cresswell, eds. *Quaternary Studies*, 21–34. Wellington: Royal Society of New Zealand.

Jones, Rhys and Jim Bowler (1980). Struggle for the savanna: Northern Australia in ecological and prehistoric perspective. In Rhys Jones, ed. *Northern Australia: Options and Implications*, 3–31. Canberra: Research School of Pacific Studies, Australian National University.

Jones, Rhys and Betty Meehan (1997). *Balmarrk wana*: Big winds of Arnhem Land. In Eric Webb, ed. *Windows on Meteorology: Australian Perspective*, 14–19. Canberra: CSIRO.

Jones, Rhys and Betty Meehan (1989). Plant foods of the Gidjingarli: Ethnographic and archaeological perspectives from northern Australia on tuber and seed exploitation. In David Harris and Gordon Hillman, eds. *Foraging and Farming: The Evolution of Plant Exploitation*. London: Unwin Hyman.

Jones, Rhys and Betty Meehan (1977). Floating bark and hollow trunks. *Hemisphere* 21: 16–21.

McKenzie, Kim (1980). *Waiting for Harry*. Documentary. Canberra: Australian Institute of Aboriginal Studies.

Meehan, Betty (1995). The *Anbarra* Archaeological Project 1970 – present. In Iain Davidson, Christine Lovell-Jones and Robyne Bancroft, eds. *Archaeologists and Aborigines Working Together*, 38–40. Armidale: University of New England Press.

Meehan, Betty (1994). Introduction. In Claudia Haagen, ed. *Bush Toys: Aboriginal Children at Play*, vii–ix. Canberra: Aboriginal Studies Press.

Meehan, Betty (1991). Wetland hunters: Some reflections. In Christopher Haynes, Michael Ridpath and Martin Williams, eds. *Monsoonal Australia: Landscape, Ecology and Man in the Northern Lowlands*, 197–206. Rotterdam: A.A. Balkema.

Meehan, Betty (1989). Plant use in contemporary Aboriginal communities and prehistoric implications. In Wendy Beck, Anne Clarke and Lesley Head, eds. *Plants in Australian Archaeology*, 14–30. Tempus 1. Archaeology and Material Culture Studies in Anthropology. St Lucia: University of Queensland.

Meehan, Betty (1988a). Changes in Aboriginal exploitation of wetlands in northern Australia. In Deborah Wade-Marshall and Peter Loveday, eds. *Floodplains Research*, vol. 2, *Northern Australia: Progress and Prospects*, Appendix 2, 1–23. Darwin: North Australia Research Unit, Australian National University.

Meehan, Betty (1988b). The "dinner time" camp: Its uses and abuses in archaeological interpretation. In Betty Meehan and Rhys Jones, eds. *Archaeology with Ethnography: An Australian Perspective*, 171–81. Proceedings of the 1983 Australian Archaeological Association Conference in Canberra. Canberra: Department of Prehistory, Research School of Pacific Studies, Australian National University.

Meehan, Betty (1986). The dreaming shellfish. *Hilton Australia* 1(5): 52–5.

Meehan, Betty (1985). Bandeiyama: She keeps going. In Isobel White, Diane Barwick and Betty Meehan, eds. *Fighters and Singers: The Lives of Some Aboriginal Women*, 200–13. Melbourne: Allen & Unwin.

Meehan, Betty (1983). A matter of choice? Some thoughts on shell gathering strategies in northern Australia. In Juliet Clutton-Brock and Caroline Grigson, eds. *Animals and Archaeology: Shell Middens, Fishes and Birds*, 3–17. Oxford: British Archaeological Reports.

Meehan, Betty (1982a). *Shell Bed to Shell Midden*. Canberra: Australian Institute of Aboriginal Studies.

Meehan, Betty (1982b). "Ten fish for one man": Some *Anbarra* attitudes towards food and health. In Janice Reid, ed. *Body, Land and Spirit: Health and Healing in Aboriginal Society*, 96–120. St Lucia: Queensland University Press.

Meehan, Betty (1980a). Nutrition and storage: Some further notes on Aboriginal use of *Pandanus* in northern Australia. *Occasional Papers in Anthropology* 10: 23–4. St Lucia: University of Queensland.

Meehan, Betty (1980b). A return to the land and traditional life. *Uniterra: United Nations Environment Programme* 5(4): 4–5.

Meehan, Betty (1980c). Who feeds the multitude? The contribution women make to the diet of Aborigines in tropical Australia. *Women in Food Chains*, 13–19. Melbourne Food Justice Centre of Friends of the Earth.

Meehan, Betty (1977a). Hunters by the seashore. *Journal of Human Evolution* 6(4): 363–70.

Meehan, Betty (1977b). Man does not live by calories alone: The role of shellfish in a coastal cuisine. In Jim Allen, Jack Golson and Rhys Jones, eds. *Sunda and Sahul: Prehistoric Studies in Southeast Asia, Melanesia and Australia*, 493–531. London: Academic Press.

Meehan, Betty (1977c). The role of seafood in the economy of a contemporary Aboriginal society in coastal Arnhem Land. Joint Select Committee on Aboriginal Land Rights in the Northern Territory. *Hansard*, 1085–95. Canberra: Government Printer.

Meehan, Betty (1975) Shell Bed to Shell Midden. Unpublished PhD thesis, Canberra: Australian National University.

Meehan, Betty and Rhys Jones (2005). Stone tool use in land with no stone: Ethnographic notes from the *Gu-jinarliya*. In Ingereth MacFarlane, Mary Jane Mountain and Robert Payton, eds. *Many Exchanges: Archaeology, History, Community and the Work* of *Isabel McBryde*, 147–69. Aboriginal History Monograph 11. Canberra: ANU Press.

Meehan, Betty and Rhys Jones (1986a). From *Anadjerramiwa* to Canberra. In Stephen Wild, ed. *Rom: An Aboriginal Ritual of Diplomacy*, 3–31. Canberra: Australian Institute of Aboriginal Studies.

Meehan, Betty and Rhys Jones (1986b). Hunter-gatherer diet: An archaeological perspective and ethnographic method. In T. Geoffrey Taylor and N.K. Jenkins, eds. *Proceedings of the XIII International Congress of Nutrition*, 951–5. London: John Libbey.

Meehan, Betty and Rhys Jones (1982). *Ngatja*: The role of the toxic plant *Cycas media* in Aboriginal secular and ceremonial life. *Toxicon* 20: 40. Oxford: Pergamon Press.

Meehan, Betty and Rhys Jones (1980). The outstation movement and hints of a white backlash. In Rhys Jones, ed. *Northern Australia: Options and Implications*, 131–57. Canberra: Research School of Pacific Studies, Australian National University.

Meehan, Betty and Rhys Jones (1978). An-barra concept of colour. In Lester Hiatt, ed. *Australian Aboriginal Concepts*, 20–39. Canberra: Australian Institute of Aboriginal Studies.

Meehan, Betty, Rhys Jones and Annie Vincent (1999). *Gula-kula*: Dogs in Anbarra Society, Arnhem Land. In Luise Hercus and Grace Koch, eds. *Sally White Commemorative Edition. Aboriginal History* 23: 83–106. Canberra: School of Humanities, Australian National University.

Meehan, Betty, Prue Gaffey and Rhys Jones (1979). Fire to steel: Aboriginal exploitation of *Pandanus* and some wider implications. *Occasional Papers in Anthropology* 9: 73–96. St Lucia: University of Queensland.

White, Neville and Betty Meehan (1994). The importance of traditional ecological knowledge (TEK): A lens on time. In Nancy Williams, ed. *Ecologies for the Twenty-First Century: Traditional Ecological Knowledge*. Gland: International Union for Conservation of Nature and Natural Resources.

White, Neville, Betty Meehan, Lester Hiatt and Rhys Jones (1990). Demography of contemporary hunter-gatherers: Lessons from central Arnhem Land. In Neville White and Betty Meehan, eds. *Hunter-Gatherer Demography: Past and Present*, 171–85. Oceania Monograph 39. Sydney: Sydney University Press.

Appendix 2

SHELLFISH RESOURCES

Shellfish species found archaeologically and their habitats (after Bourke 2012; Brockwell 2013; Faulkner 2013; Meehan 1982a, but with nomenclature of families and species updated to March 2025 by Richard Willan).

* Species eaten by *Gu-jingarliya* between July 1972 and July 1973 (Meehan, 1982a, 179–81).

Family	Species	*Gu-jingarliya* name	Habitat
Arcidae	*Tegillarca granosa** *Trisidos* sp.	*Ngandipurdurda*	Littoral sand and mud Sublittoral sand
Cyrenoididae	*Geloina erosa**	*An-bambula; An-gailitja*	Mangrove mud
Ellobiidae	*Cassidula angulifera*	*Rrarramunbar, Belminbar*	Mangrove mud (*Rhizophora/Bruguiera*)
Mactridae	*Mactra abbreviata**	*Mu-ralkara*	Sublittoral sand
Melongenidae	*Volegalea cochlidium** (syn. *Volegalea wardiana*)*	*An-jalabaykarda*	Sand and mud in shallow water
Mesodesmatidae	*Coecella horsfieldii*		Intertidal coarse sand
Mytilidae	*Modiolus proclivis*	*Ngalpur*	Sand and mud in shallow water/estuaries
Nassariidae	*Nassarius dorsatus*	*An-ganena*	Sandy mudflats
Naticidae	*Neverita didyma**	*An-jiderda, Rang-go, ngulkiyarra*	Sandy mudflats
Neritidae	*Nerita balteata**	*Ana-jima*	Middle intertidal zone of mangroves
Ostreidae	*Saccostrea scyphophilla**	An-guljuraba	Mid-intertidal rocks

Family	**Species**	***Gu-jingarliya* name**	**Habitat**
Potamididae	*Cerithidea anticipata*	*Rrarramunbar, Belminbar*	Shallow mud/mangrove roots (*Avicennia, Bruguiera*)
	*Telescopium Telescopium**	*Nornda*	Mangroves (*Rhizophora*)
	*Terebralia palustris**	*Ana-mula an-ika*	Mangroves (*Avicennia, Bruguiera, Ceriops*)
Tellinidae	*Tellina* sp.	*An-demburela*	Littoral sands and muds
Turbinellidae	*Syrinx aruana**	*An-jalabaykarda*	Sublittoral/intertidal zone
Veneridae	*Dosinia* sp.*	*An-dirrbula*	Sandy mudflats
	*Marcia hiantina**	*Diyama*	Littoral sand and mudflats
	Placamen sp.	*An-dirrbula*	Sublittoral sand
Volutidae	*Melo amphora**	*An-gujawiya*	Sandy mudflats
	*Cymbiola flavicans**	*Ana-jirralanggula*	Sandy mudflats

INDEX

Aboriginal Areas Protection Authority xxiii
Adelaide River 81
Agajang-guwa (*Agadjang-guwa*) xvi, 25, 74
  chronology 27
  sampling 27
  site description 27
Anadara andtiquata 52
Anajerramiwa (*Anadjerramiwa*) xvi
Anamanba (*Anandamamba*) xvi, 13, 25, 75, 76
  chronology 27
  map 14
  sampling 27
  site description 27
  soil samples 17
Ana-nganandak (*Ananganandark*) xvi
An-barra Archaeological Project 6, 7–9, 86
  aim 8–9
  chronology 26, 28–9
  ethnographic evidence 82–4, 86
  fieldwork 19–23
  genetic research 85–6
  laboratory analysis 23–4
  linguistic evidence 84–5, 86
  map of sites 26
  material, repatriation of 23
  methodology 19–24
  results, presentation of 24
  sampling and excavation 23
  significance 9
  sites 25–6, 73
An-barra text
  English 87–96
  Gu-jingarliya 97–105
Andakul 40
an-dirrbula 92–6 *see also Dosinia*
Angabarapara, Les 36
angalidjauwurigia 80
An-gartcha Wana (*Angatja Wana*, Blyth River) xvi, xix, xx, xxii–xxv, 1, 2, 5, 6, 82
  aerial view 12
  archaeological project *see An-barra* Archaeological Project
  climate
    change 80–1
    current 18–19
    Holocene 11–13, 80–1
  colonial exploration 5
  environmental zones (map) 19
  geomorphological fieldwork 13–17
  landscape
    changing nature of 78–9
    current 18–19, 79
    Holocene 11–13
  location 11
an-guljaraba 52
Aningarra, Michael 27, 92
Aningarra's Camp xvi, 25, 74, 79, 92, 101
  chronology 30
  excavation 30
  results 30
  site description 27, 30
Ankin, Shereen 98
Anmal Mandayerra 13
  map 14
  soil samples 13, 17
Anuru Bay 7

Arafura Sea 4, 11, 87
Arafura Swamp 6
archaeological investigations xxi–xxii, xxiii–xxv, 6–7
  An-barra Archaeological Project *see An-barra* Archaeological Project
  limitations 1
  map of sites 26
  material, repatriation of 23
  sites 25–6
archaeology
  ethnography, and 82–4, 86
Archaeology and Natural History (ANH), School of Culture, History and Language 8
Archaeology with Ethnography: An Australian Perspective 82
Arnhem Land xix, xxii, 8, 11, 81, 85, 86, 92
  archaeological investigations 6–7
  trepang harvesting 3–4
arrack 4
art xxi, 90
  rock 6, 7
Australian Institute of Aboriginal and Torres Strait Islander Studies (AIATSIS) xxiv
  funding 20
Australian Institute of Aboriginal Studies (AIAS) xxiii
Australian National University (ANU)
  Radiocarbon Laboratory 26
  storage facility 7–8
Australian trepang fishers
  contact with 4

Ballard, Chris 82
Balpilja Swamp 13, 14, 17, 21, 27, 41, 76, 79, 90, 93
Bandeiyama, Nancy xx, xxiii, 7, 21, 90, 91
banyan (*Ficus virens*) 70
barra 84
barramundi (*Lates calcarifer*) 46
Beck, Associate Professor Wendy xxiii
Bedford, Stuart 82
Bell, Curly xix, 6, 87
Bennett, Dorothy 90, 91
Big Swamp Phase 14, 17
Blue Mud Bay 6, 73, 81, 85
Blyth River *see An-gartcha Wana*
Bolgunirra-gaboiya xvi
Boucaut Bay xix, 5, 11, 87
Bourke, Dr Patricia 21
Brockwell, Sally xxii, xxiv, 8, 92
  fieldwork 20–3
  results, presentation of 24
Burama, Ernie 98
Burarra 84, 85

Cadell River 6, 18
Canberra bushfires 7–8
Cape Stewart xv, 5, 7, 11
Cape York 78, 81
Carew, Margaret, xv, 84
Carmichael, Bethune 21, 51–2
Carrington, Captain 5
Cassidula 41
Centre for Archaeological Research at ANU (CAR) 26
Centre for Indigenous Natural and Cultural Resource Management 22
ceremonies xxi, 3, 5
  Rom ceremony xxiii, xxiv
Cerithidea 41
Cerithidea anticipata 74
Chappell, John 13–17, 92
Chelodina rugosa 75
chenier ridges 12
climate
  current 18–19
  Holocene 11–13, 21, 52, 80–1
Coburg Peninsula 4, 7
Coecella horsfieldii 75
Colman, Dr Philip 23
contacts 3
  Australian trepang fishers 4
  Europeans post-1940 6
  Europeans pre-1940 5
  Japanese pearl fishers 4–5
  Macassans 3–4
continuity 79–80, 86
Coombs, Dr Herbert Cole "Nugget" 89
Cuthbertson, Walter 5
Cycas media 70
Cymbiola 41, 69

Darwin xix, 8, 81, 87
  fieldwork 21–3

datcho (cake) 60
"dead men" sites 9, 77–8, 84, 86
dinner time camps 82
diyama 40–1, 52, 93
Djambidj song series xxiii, 3
Djinbor, Nancy 21
Djomi Museum xxiv
Djowanga 70
Dosinia 31, 33, 40, 41, 53, 56–8, 64, 65, 69, 74–5, 81, 92
  charcoal pair 30, 39, 51, 56, 71
  Dosinia juvenilis 23, 27, 36, 44, 52, 57, 68, 71, 75, 77, 79
Dreaming 83, 92, 93
  white ochre 40, 93
"Dreaming" sites 9, 32, 77–8, 83–4
Drysdale, David 6
Drysdale, Ingrid 6

earth mounds (*gun-gapula*) 6, 8, 20, 73, 74, 75–6, 86 *see also by name of site*
Egan, Ted 6
El Niño Southern Oscillation (ENSO) 12
Eleocharis swamp 17
Epi 82
ethnography 86
  interpretive tool, as 82–4
Eucalyptus tetradonta 18
Europeans, contact with
  post-1940 6
  pre-1940 5

faunal material
  identification of 23–4
fieldwork 19–23
food resources xx–xxi, 18–19
  environment, impact of, 3, 9
fork-tailed catfish (*Arius* sp.) 46
Freshwater Phase 13, 17
Fry, George 34, 35
funerary practices 2

Galpadanga, Tommy 36
gangula (Arafura palm) 60
Garawun, George xxiii
Geloina 23, 41, 69
  Geloina coaxans (mangrove mud whelk) 76
genetic research 85–6
geomorphology 13–17, 85
Gidjingali xv, 4, 70, 79
  division of 7
Gindjerakama, Elva 98
Girrirrwanga, Barney 93
Glasgow, Kathleen xv
Gochan Jiny-jirra 94
Goulburn Island 5
Goyulan song series 3
Groote Eylandt 7
Gu-jingarliya xv, 6, 76, 84
  Japanese, contact with 5
Gulukula (*Kula Kula*) xvi, 25, 51, 75, 77, 79, 80, 83, 93, 101–2
  chronology 33
  Dog Mounds 32, 93
  excavation 13, 17, 33
  map 14
  results 33
  site description 32
  soil samples 13, 17
Gumugun, Sam xxiii
Guna-jengga (*Gunedjanga*) xvi, 25, 32, 73, 74, 77–80, 93, 102
  chronology 39
  fish-trap 33–6
  results 39–40
  sampling 38–9
  site description 36–8
Gunavidji (*Ndjebbana*) 4–5
Gun-nartpa 76
  dialect xv
Gupanga (*Kopanga*) xvi, xx–xxi, 4, 21, 25, 27, 34, 61, 77, 79, 90, 94, 95
Gupanga wangarr an-dakal a-yurra 40–1, 93, 102
  chronology 41
Gurrmanamana, Frank xx, xxi, xxiii, 4, 7, 21, 41, 89, 93–4
  Dog Mounds, description of 32
  song series xxiii
Guyoyo xvi

Hiatt, Les xv, xix–xx, xxii, xxiv, 6, 87, 89–90, 91
Holocene 6, 7, 8, 9, 73
  climate change 11–13, 21, 52, 80–1, 86
  economic and social change 82
  landscape change 11–13, 86

Japanese pearl fishers
contact with 4–5
jarrka (goanna) 60
Ji-bena (*Djibena*) xvi, xxi, 2, 21, 25, 27, 41, 75–6, 81, 86, 93–4, 102–3
chronology 41
excavation 41
faunal material 44, 46, 47–9
map 14
results 41–6
shell taxa 41–4, 45–6
soil samples 8, 13, 17
stone assemblage 46, 49–50
Jilangga a-jirra (*Djilangadjerra*) xvi, 46, 74, 94, 103
chronology 51
sampling 51
Jimarda 94
Jinawunya (*Djunawunya, Djunawinia*) xvi, xxiii, 4, 21, 25, 27, 34, 51–2, 74, 78–9, 94, 103
chronology 52
map 14
soil samples 13, 17
Jindjerakama, Elva 92
jin-gombula (mouse) 60
Jones, Rhys xv, xx–xxv, 6, 39, 42, 62, 90, 92
An-barra Archaeological Project *see An-barra* Archaeological Project
community, living with xx–xxi, 6, 18–19, 21
geomorphological fieldwork 13–17
research trips xxii–xxv, 7
Jurnarka (*Djunaka, Djinaka*) xvi, 25, 34, 52, 73, 74, 94, 103–4
chronology 53
excavation 53
results 53, 54
sampling 53

Kakadu 7
kapal (black soil plains) 60
Kaprys, The xix, 87
Keon-Cohen, Dr Bryan xxiii
King, Captain Philip Parker 5
Kunibidji country 87
Kupang (Koepang) 4
Kuwae 82, 86

La Niña conditions 13
laboratory analysis 23–4
Lalarr gu-jirrapa (*Lalar-gadjirrapa, Lalagidjiripa, Lalargedjiripa*) xvi, xxi, 25, 34, 37, 74, 79, 90
Lampert, Dr Ronald xxiii
landscape
changing nature of 78–9
current 18–19, 79
Holocene 11–13
Larkun Adjiripa (place of the coffin) 54–5
Last Glacial Maximum 11
Lawuk a-jirrapa (stone-spear-point-place) 70, 76
Lindsay, David 5
linguistic evidence 84–5, 86
Litster, Dr Mirani 21
Little Ice Age 82
Liverpool River xix, 5, 11
Lorrkon a-jirrapa (*Larrakun-adjirrapa*) xvi, 25, 54–6, 74, 79, 95, 104
East/West 1974 54–6
chronology 56
results 56
sampling 56
map 14
sampling 13, 17
West 1978 56–8
chronology 57
excavation 56–7
results 57–8, 59
sampling 56–7

Macassans 6
contact with 3–4
McKenzie, Kim xiii
Mactra 30, 33, 36, 41, 64, 68, 70–1, 74, 92
Madai 37
Madangadjire 35
Madayjapa (*Madaidjapa*) xvi
Malkorda, Frank xxiii
Malmilajerra (*Malmiladjerra*) xvi
mangroves 13
freshwater wetlands, change to 17
species 30, 31, 74
Maningrida xix–xx, xxii, xxiv, 8, 11, 78
burials 2
establishment 6

field trips 20–1, 87–90
school xx, xxii, 89–90
map of study area 2
Marcia 23, 30, 40, 41, 52, 64, 68, 69, 81, 93
Marcia hiantina 74, 79
Mason, Dominic xxii, 21, 98
Matai (*Martay*) 58, 60, 73, 77, 78, 95
Meehan, Betty xv, xix, 4, 6, 88, 91
An-barra Archaeological Project *see An-barra* Archaeological Project
An-barra text *see An-barra* text
community, living with xix–xxi, 6, 9, 18–19, 21
research trips xxii–xxv, 7, 8
studies xx–xxi
Melo amphora 41
Melongenidae 69
Methodist Overseas Mission 5
methodology 19–24
fieldwork 19–23
laboratory analysis 23–4
results, presentation of 24
sampling and excavation 23
Miadjirripa 61, 68, 80
middens 6, 8, 20
shell *see* shell middens
Milikins, Trevor 6
Milingimbi 5, 78
Minjambilamirra (*Mindjambilamirra*) xvi
Modiolus 33, 41, 56, 70
Modiolus modulaides 74
Moffat, Dr Ian 21
monsoonal climate 18
Mugamandija (*Mugamandidja*) xvi
Mu-ganarra (*Moganarra, Moganara*) xvi, 79
Mu-garnbal (*Maganbal*) xvii, 25, 58, 60, 73–4, 78, 84, 86, 95, 104
chronology 60
results 60
sampling 60
Mu-lela (*Milela*) xvii
Mulumbuk, Harry 93
Museum and Art Gallery of the Northern Territory (MAGNT) 8, 9, 22–4, 26, 76
material, repatriation of 23
Muyu a-jirrapa (*Moiya-adjirripa*) xvii, 21, 25, 74, 80, 95, 104
Coastal Shell Midden 1974 75
chronology 65
excavation (1978) 64–5
photos 62–3
results 65–7
sampling (1974) 64
site description 61
survey (1978) 64–5
Shell Mound 1974/1978 8, 75
chronology 68
excavation (1978) 68
results 69
sampling (1974) 68
site description 68

Nassarius 41
Native Title Claim xxiv
Ndjebbana xix
Neverita 41
New Guinea 11
Ngakunal-yorda xvii
Ngalpura Jinyu-nirripa 2 13
map 14
soil samples 14, 17
Ngalpura Jinyu-nirripa 3 13
map 14
soil samples 14, 17
Ngan-galala plains 78
Nganyjuwa (*Ngandjuwa*) xvii
Ngarli ji-bama (*Ngalidjibama*) xvii, 25, 74, 77, 95, 104–5
chronology 70
results 71
sampling 70
site description 70
Ngarrabullgan 81
Ngurrpangurrpa, Betty xxi, xxii, xxiv, xxv, 7, 13, 20, 21, 52, 90, 92, 98
northern brown bandicoot (*Isoodon macrourus*) 44, 75
northern brushtail possum (*Trichosurus arnhemensis*) 44, 75
Northern Land Council xxiv
NT Sacred Sites Authority xxiii
Nusa Tenggara 4

occupation of land 1–3
outstation movement 6
oysters (*Saccostrea*) 52, 69

Pandanus 70
  nuts 51, 94
Pandanus spiralis (Screw palm) xxiii
People of the Rivermouth xxiv, 20
Places in Peril – Archaeology in the Anthropocene 21, 52
Placuna 68
Pleistocene 7, 14
  post-Pleistocene sea-level rise 11
Ponder, Dr Winston 23

Rankin, Stewart 13, 92
religion xxi, 3, 5
results, presentation of 24
Robinson, Edwin 5, 7
rock shelters 6, 7
Rom ceremony xxiii, xxiv
rrawa (remembered camp site) 33, 77, 90, 92–5

Saccostrea 41, 68
saline mudflats 13
scholarship, previous 2–3
Scougall, Dr Stuart 90
Searcy, Alfred 5
secondary burial 2
Shell Bed to Shell Midden xxi, 8, 20, 25, 86
shell middens 6, 8, 20, 73–4, 86 *see also by name of site*
  ethnographic analogy and mythology 83
  mounds, distinguished 77
shell mounds 6, 7, 8, 20, 73, 75, 86 *see also by name of site*
  middens, distinguished 77
shell rock 40–1
shellfish resources 127–8
soil sampling 23
song series xxiii, 3
spelling xv
Sterculia quadrifolia 70
Stewart, Freda 23
stone assemblage 46, 49–50, 76
Strangman, Cecil 5
summary of contact xxii–xxv
Sweeney, Gordon 5, 6
Syrinx 41, 64

Tamarindus indica (*jambang*) 4
Tarbett-Buckley, Dr Christine 22
Tegillarca 23, 41, 69, 78, 81
  Tegillarca granosa 74
Telescopium 23, 41, 69, 76
  Telescopium telescopium 74
Tellina 41, 69
Terebralia 23, 41, 69, 95
  Terebralia palustris 74
Terminalia carpentariae 70
Thomson, David 5
tobacco 4
Tongoa 82
Torres Strait 11, 81
Transition Phase 13, 17
trepang (*burnapi*) 3
turtles 44, 75, 76, 93
  long-necked 75

Ussher, Dr Ella 23

Vanderlin Island 7
Vanuatu 82
  volcanic eruption 82, 86
Volegalea 41
Volema 41

Waikato Radiocarbon Dating Laboratory 26
Waiting for Harry (film) xxiii
Webb, Reverend T.T. 5
Weipa 73, 78, 81
Wellington Range 7
whistle duck 41
Willan, Dr Richard 23
Woodward Commission 6

Xanthomelon 41

yams (*Dioscorea*) 70
Yolngu 85
Yuluk a-jirrapa (*Yuluk-adjirrapa*) xvii, 25, 71, 75, 77, 83, 96, 105
  chronology 71
  results 71
  sampling 71

www.ingramcontent.com/pod-product-compliance
Lightning Source LLC
Chambersburg PA
CBHW040247290326
41929CB00054B/3451

9781761540202